CAKE COOKBOOK 2022

A GREAT SELECTION OF DELICIOUS RECIPES

FOR BEGINNERS

MARTHA WILLIAMS

Table of Contents

Strawberry Mousse Gâteau 12

Yule Log 14

Easter Bonnet Cake 16

Easter Simnel Cake 17

Twelfth Night Cake 19

Microwave Apple Cake 20

Microwave Applesauce Cake 21

Microwave Apple and Walnut Cake 22

Microwave Carrot Cake 23

Microwave Carrot, Pineapple and Nut Cake 24

Microwave Spiced Bran Cakes 26

Microwave Banana and Passion Fruit Cheesecake 27

Microwave Baked Orange Cheesecake 28

Microwave Pineapple Cheesecake 29

Microwave Cherry and Nut Loaf 30

Microwave Chocolate Cake 31

Microwave Chocolate Almond Cake 32

Microwave Double Chocolate Brownies 34

Microwave Chocolate Date Bars 35

Microwave Chocolate Squares 36

Microwave Quick Coffee Cake 37

Microwave Christmas Cake 38

Microwave Crumb Cake 40

Microwave Date Bars 41

Microwave Fig Bread 42

Microwave Flapjacks 43

Microwave Fruit Cake 44

Microwave Fruit and Coconut Squares 45

Microwave Fudge Cake 46

Microwave Gingerbread 47

Microwave Ginger Bars 48

Microwave Golden Cake 49

Microwave Honey and Hazelnut Cake 50

Microwave Chewy Muesli Bars 51

Microwave Nut Cake 52

Microwave Orange Juice Cake 53

Microwave Pavlova 54

Microwave Shortcake 55

Microwave Strawberry Shortcake 56

Microwave Sponge Cake 57

Microwave Sultana Bars 58

Microwave Chocolate Biscuits 59

Microwave Coconut Cookies 60

Microwave Florentines 61

Microwave Hazelnut and Cherry Biscuits 62

Microwave Sultana Biscuits 63

Microwave Banana Bread 64

Microwave Cheese Bread 65

Microwave Walnut Loaf 66

No-bake Amaretti Cake 67

American Crispy Rice Bars 68

Apricot Squares 69

Apricot Swiss Roll Cake 70

Broken Biscuit Cakes 71

No-bake Buttermilk Cake 72

Chestnut Slice 73

Chestnut Sponge Cake 74

Chocolate and Almond Bars 76

Chocolate Crisp Cake 77

Chocolate Crumb Squares 78

Chocolate Fridge Cake 79

Chocolate and Fruit Cake 80

Chocolate and Ginger Squares 81

Luxury Chocolate and Ginger Squares 82

Honey Chocolate Cookies 83

Chocolate Layer Cake 84

Nice Chocolate Bars 85

Chocolate Praline Squares 86

Coconut Crunchies 87

Crunch Bars 88

Coconut and Raisin Crunchies 89

Coffee Milk Squares 90

No-bake Fruit Cake 91

Fruity Squares 92

Fruit and Fibre Crackles 93

Nougat Layer Cake 94

Milk and Nutmeg Squares 95

Muesli Crunch 97

Orange Mousse Squares ... 98

Peanut Squares ... 99

Peppermint Caramel Cakes ... 100

Rice Cookies ... 101

Rice and Chocolate Toffette ... 102

Almond Paste ... 103

Sugar-free Almond Paste ... 104

Royal Icing ... 105

Sugar-free Icing ... 106

Fondant Icing ... 107

Butter Icing ... 108

Chocolate Butter Icing ... 109

White Chocolate Butter Icing ... 110

Coffee Butter Icing ... 111

Lemon Butter Icing ... 112

Orange Butter Icing ... 113

Cream Cheese Icing ... 114

Orange Icing ... 115

Orange Liqueur Icing ... 116

Oat and Raisin Cookies ... 117

Spiced Oatmeal Biscuits ... 118

Wholemeal Oat Biscuits ... 119

Orange Biscuits ... 120

Orange and Lemon Biscuits ... 121

Orange and Walnut Biscuits ... 122

Orange and Chocolate Chip Biscuits ... 123

Spiced Orange Biscuits ... 124

Peanut Butter Biscuits 125

Peanut Butter and Chocolate Swirls 126

Oaty Peanut Butter Biscuits 127

Honey and Coconut Peanut Butter Biscuits 128

Pecan Nut Biscuits 129

Pinwheel Biscuits 130

Quick Buttermilk Biscuits 131

Raisin Biscuits 132

Soft Raisin Biscuits 133

Raisin and Treacle Slices 134

Ratafia Biscuits 135

Rice and Muesli Cookies 136

Romany Creams 137

Sand Biscuits 138

Soured Cream Cookies 139

Brown Sugar Biscuits 140

Sugar and Nutmeg Biscuits 141

Shortbread 142

Christmas Shortbread 143

Honeyed Shortbread 144

Lemon Shortbread 145

Mincemeat Shortbread 146

Nut Shortbread 147

Orange Shortbread 148

Rich Man's Shortbread 149

Wholemeal Oat Shortbread 150

Almond Whirls 151

Chocolate Meringue Shortbread	152
Biscuit People	153
Iced Ginger Shortcake	154
Shrewsbury Biscuits	155
Spanish Spiced Biscuits	156
Old-fashioned Spice Biscuits	157
Treacle Biscuits	158
Treacle, Apricot and Nut Cookies	159
Treacle and Buttermilk Cookies	160
Treacle and Coffee Biscuits	161
Treacle and Date Cookies	162
Treacle and Ginger Cookies	163
Vanilla Biscuits	164
Walnut Biscuits	165
Crisp Biscuits	166
Cheddar Biscuits	167
Blue Cheese Biscuits	168
Cheese and Sesame Biscuits	169
Cheese Straws	170
Cheese and Tomato Biscuits	171
Goats' Cheese Bites	172
Ham and Mustard Rolls	173
Ham and Pepper Biscuits	174
Simple Herb Biscuits	175
Indian Biscuits	176
Hazelnut and Shallot Shortbread	177
Salmon and Dill Biscuits	178

Soda Biscuits	179
Tomato and Parmesan Pinwheels	180
Tomato and Herb Biscuits	181
Basic White Loaf	182
Bagels	183
Baps	184
Creamy Barley Loaf	185
Beer Bread	186
Boston Brown Bread	187
Bran Flowerpots	188
Buttered Rolls	189
Buttermilk Loaf	190
Canadian Corn Bread	191
Cornish Rolls	192
Country Flat Bread	193
Country Poppyseed Plait	194
Country Wholemeal Bread	195
Curry Plaits	196
Devon Splits	198
Fruited Wheatgerm Bread	199
Fruity Milk Plaits	200
Granary Bread	201
Granary Rolls	202
Granary Bread with Hazelnuts	203
Grissini	204
Harvest Plait	205
Milk Bread	207

Milk Fruit Loaf 208

Morning Glory Bread.. 209

Muffin Bread 210

No-rise Bread 211

Pizza Dough 212

Oatmeal Cob 213

Oatmeal Farl.. 214

Pitta Bread 215

Quick Brown Bread 216

Moist Rice Bread 217

Rice and Almond Loaf 218

Strawberry Mousse Gâteau

Makes one 23 cm/9 in cake

For the cake:

100 g/4 oz/1 cup self-raising (self-rising) flour

100 g/4 oz/½ cup butter or margarine, softened

100 g/4 oz/½ cup caster (superfine) sugar

2 eggs

For the mousse:

15 ml/1 tbsp powdered gelatine

30 ml/2 tbsp water

450 g/1 lb strawberries

3 eggs, separated

75 g/3 oz/1/3 cup caster (superfine) sugar

5 ml/1 tsp lemon juice

300 ml/½ pt/1¼ cups double (heavy) cream

30 ml/2 tbsp flaked (slivered) almonds, lightly toasted

Beat together the cake ingredients until smooth. Spoon into a greased and lined 23 cm/9 in cake tin (pan) and bake in a preheated oven at 190°C/375°F/gas mark 5 for 25 minutes until golden brown and firm to the touch. Remove from the tin and leave to cool.

To make the mousse, sprinkle the gelatine over the water in a bowl and leave until spongy. Stand the bowl in a pan of hot water and leave until dissolved. Leave to cool slightly. Meanwhile, purée 350 g/12 oz of the strawberries, then rub through a sieve (strainer) to discard the pips. Beat the egg yolks and sugar until pale and thick and the mixture trails off the whisk in ribbons. Stir in the purée, lemon juice and gelatine. Whip the cream until stiff, then fold half into the mixture. With a clean whisk and bowl, whisk the egg whites until stiff, then fold into the mixture.

Cut the sponge in half horizontally and place one half in the base of a clean cake tin (pan) lined with clingfilm (plastic wrap). Slice the remaining strawberries and arrange over the sponge, then top with the flavoured cream, and finally the second layer of cake. Press down very gently. Chill until set.

To serve, invert the gâteau on to a serving plate and remove the clingfilm (plastic wrap). Decorate with the remaining cream and garnish with the almonds.

Yule Log

Makes one

3 eggs

100 g/4 oz/½ cup caster (superfine) sugar

100 g/4 oz/1 cup plain (all-purpose) flour

50 g/2 oz/½ cup plain (semi-sweet) chocolate, grated

15 ml/1 tbsp hot water

Caster (superfine) sugar for rolling

For the icing (frosting):

175 g/6 oz/¾ cup butter or margarine, softened

350 g/12 oz/2 cups icing (confectioners') sugar, sifted

30 ml/2 tbsp warm water

30 ml/2 tbsp cocoa (unsweetened chocolate) powder To decorate:

Holly leaves and robin (optional)

Beat together the eggs and sugar in a heatproof bowl set over a pan of gently simmering water. Continue to beat until the mixture is stiff and trails off the whisk in ribbons. Remove from the heat and beat until cool. Fold in half the flour, then the chocolate, then the remaining flour, then stir in the water. Spoon into a greased and lined Swiss roll tin (jelly roll pan) and bake in a preheated oven at 220°C/425°F/gas mark 7 for about 10 minutes until firm to the touch. Sprinkle a large sheet of greaseproof (waxed) paper with caster sugar. Turn the cake out of the tin on to the paper and trim the edges. Cover with another sheet of paper and roll up loosely from the short edge.

To make the icing, cream together the butter or margarine and icing sugar, then beat in the water and cocoa. Unroll the cold cake, remove the paper and spread the cake with half the icing. Roll it up again, then ice with the remaining icing, marking it with a fork to look like a log. Sift a little icing sugar over the top and decorate as liked.

Easter Bonnet Cake

Makes one 20 cm/8 in cake

75 g/3 oz/1/3 cup muscovado sugar

3 eggs

75 g/3 oz/¾ cup self-raising (self-rising) flour

15 ml/1 tbsp cocoa (unsweetened chocolate) powder

15 ml/1 tbsp warm water

For the filling:
50 g/2 oz/¼ cup butter or margarine, softened

75 g/3 oz/½ cup icing (confectioners') sugar, sifted

For the topping:
100 g/4 oz/1 cup plain (semi-sweet) chocolate

25 g/1 oz/2 tbsp butter or margarine

Ribbon or sugar flowers (optional)

Beat together the sugar and eggs in a heatproof bowl set over a pan of gently simmering water. Continue to beat until the mixture is thick and creamy. Leave to stand for a few minutes, then remove from the heat and beat again until the mixture leaves a trail when the whisk is removed. Fold in the flour and cocoa, then stir in the water. Spoon the mixture into a greased and lined 20 cm/8 in cake tin (pan) and a greased and lined 15 cm/ 6 in cake tin. Bake in a preheated oven at 200°C/400°F/gas mark 6 for 15–20 minutes until well risen and firm to the touch. Leave to cool on a wire rack.

To make the filling, cream together the margarine and icing sugar. Use to sandwich the smaller cake on top of the larger one.

To make the topping, melt the chocolate and butter or margarine in a heatproof bowl set over a pan of gently simmering water. Spoon the topping over the cake and spread with a knife dipped in hot water so that it is completely covered. Decorate round the brim with a ribbon or sugar flowers.

Easter Simnel Cake

Makes one 20 cm/8 in cake

225 g/8 oz/1 cup butter or margarine, softened

225 g/8 oz/1 cup soft brown sugar

Grated rind of 1 lemon

4 eggs, beaten

225 g/8 oz/2 cups plain (all-purpose) flour

5 ml/1 tsp baking powder

2.5 ml/½ tsp grated nutmeg

50 g/2 oz/½ cup cornflour (cornstarch)

100 g/4 oz/2/3 cup sultanas (golden raisins)

100 g/4 oz/2/3 cup raisins

75 g/3 oz/½ cup currants

100 g/4 oz/½ cup glacé (candied) cherries, chopped

25 g/1 oz/¼ cup ground almonds

450 g/1 lb Almond Paste

30 ml/2 tbsp apricot jam (conserve)

1 egg white, beaten

Cream together the butter or mar- garine, sugar and lemon rind until pale and fluffy. Gradually beat in the eggs, then fold in the flour, baking powder, nutmeg and cornflour. Stir in the fruit and almonds. Spoon half the mixture into a greased and lined 20 cm/8 in deep cake tin (pan). Roll out half the almond paste to a circle the size of the cake and place on top of the mixture. Fill with the remaining mixture and bake in a pre-heated oven at 160°C/325°F/gas mark 3 for 2–2½ hours until golden brown. Leave to cool in the tin. When cool, turn out and wrap in greaseproof (waxed) paper. Store in an airtight container for up to three weeks if possible to mature.

To finish the cake, brush the top with the jam. Roll out three-quarters of the remaining almond paste to a 20 cm/8 in circle, neaten the edges and place on top of the cake. Roll the remaining almond paste into 11 balls (to represent the disciples without Judas). Brush the top of the cake with beaten egg white and arrange the balls around the edge of the cake, then brush them with egg white. Place under a hot grill (broiler) for a minute or so to brown it slightly.

Twelfth Night Cake

Makes one 20 cm/8 in cake

225 g/8 oz/1 cup butter or margarine, softened

225 g/8 oz/1 cup soft brown sugar

4 eggs, beaten

225 g/8 oz/2 cups plain (all-purpose) flour

5 ml/1 tsp ground mixed (apple-pie) spice

175 g/6 oz/1 cup sultanas (golden raisins)

100 g/4 oz/2/3 cup raisins

75 g/3 oz/½ cup currants

50 g/2 oz/¼ cup glacé (candied) cherries

50 g/2 oz/1/3 cup chopped mixed (candied) peel

30 ml/2 tbsp milk

12 candles to decorate

Cream together the butter or mar- garine and sugar until pale and fluffy. Gradually beat in the eggs, then fold in the flour, mixed spice, fruit and peel and mix until well blended, adding a little milk if necessary to achieve a soft mixture. Spoon into a greased and lined 20 cm/8 in cake tin (pan) and bake in a preheated oven at 180°C/350°F/gas mark 4 for 2 hours until a skewer inserted in the centre comes out clean. Leave

Microwave Apple Cake

Makes one 23 cm/9 in square

100 g/4 oz/½ cup butter or margarine, softened

100 g/4 oz/½ cup soft brown sugar

30 ml/2 tbsp golden (light corn) syrup

2 eggs, lightly beaten

225 g/8 oz/2 cups self-raising (self-rising) flour

10 ml/2 tsp ground mixed (apple-pie) spice

120 ml/4 fl oz/½ cup milk

2 cooking (tart) apples, peeled, cored and thinly sliced

15 ml/1 tbsp caster (superfine) sugar

5 ml/1 tsp ground cinnamon

Cream together the butter or margarine, brown sugar and syrup until pale and fluffy. Gradually beat in the eggs. Fold in the flour and mixed spice, then stir in the milk until you have a soft consistency. Stir in the apples. Spoon into a greased and base-lined 23 cm/9 in microwave ring mould (tube pan) and microwave on Medium for 12 minutes until firm. Allow to stand for 5 minutes, then turn out upside-down and sprinkle with the caster sugar and cinnamon.

Microwave Applesauce Cake

Makes one 20 cm/8 in cake

100 g/4 oz/½ cup butter or margarine, softened

175 g/6 oz/¾ cup soft brown sugar

1 egg, lightly beaten

175 g/6 oz/1½ cups plain (all-purpose) flour

2.5 ml/½ tsp baking powder

A pinch of salt

2.5 ml/½ tsp ground allspice

1.5 ml/¼ tsp grated nutmeg

1.5 ml/¼ tsp ground cloves

300 ml/½ pt/1¼ cups unsweetened apple purée (sauce)

75 g/3 oz/½ cup raisins

Icing (confectioner's) sugar for dusting

Cream together the butter or mar-garine and brown sugar until light and fluffy. Gradually beat in the egg, then fold in the flour, baking powder, salt and spices alternately with the apple purée and raisins. Spoon into a greased and floured 20 cm/8 in square microwave dish and microwave on High for 12 minutes. Leave to cool in the dish, then cut into squares and dust with icing sugar.

Microwave Apple and Walnut Cake

Makes one 20 cm/8 in cake

175 g/6 oz/¾ cup butter or margarine, softened

100 g/4 oz/½ cup caster (superfine) sugar

3 eggs, lightly beaten

30 ml/2 tbsp golden (light corn) syrup

Grated rind and juice of 1 lemon

175 g/6 oz/1½ cups self-raising (self-rising) flour

50 g/2 oz/½ cup walnuts, chopped

1 eating (dessert) apple, peeled, cored and chopped

100 g/4 oz/2/3 cup icing (confectioner's) sugar

30 ml/2 tbsp lemon juice

15 ml/1 tbsp water

Walnut halves to decorate

Cream together the butter or mar-garine and caster sugar until light and fluffy. Gradually add the eggs, then the syrup, lemon rind and juice. Fold in the flour, chopped nuts and apple. Spoon into a greased 20 cm/8 in round microwave dish and microwave on High for 4 minutes. Remove from the oven and cover with foil. Leave to cool. Mix the icing sugar with the lemon juice and enough of the water to form a smooth icing (frosting). Spread over the cake and decorate with walnut halves.

Microwave Carrot Cake

Makes one 18 cm/7 in cake

100 g/4 oz/½ cup butter or margarine, softened

100 g/4 oz/½ cup soft brown sugar

2 eggs, beaten

Grated rind and juice of 1 orange

2.5 ml/½ tsp ground cinnamon

A pinch of grated nutmeg

100 g/4 oz carrots, grated

100 g/4 oz/1 cup self-raising (self-rising) flour

25 g/1 oz/¼ cup ground almonds

25 g/1 oz/2 tbsp caster (superfine) sugar

For the topping:

100 g/4 oz/½ cup cream cheese

50 g/2 oz/1/3 cup icing (confectioners') sugar, sifted

30 ml/2 tbsp lemon juice

Cream together the butter and sugar until light and fluffy. Gradually beat in the eggs, then stir in the orange juice and rind, the spices and carrots. Fold in the flour, almonds and sugar. Spoon into a greased and lined 18 cm/7 in cake dish and cover with clingfilm (plastic wrap). Microwave on High for 8 minutes until a skewer inserted in the centre comes out clean. Remove the clingfilm and leave to stand for 8 minutes before turning out on to a wire rack to finish cooling. Beat the topping ingredients together, then spread over the cooled cake.

Microwave Carrot, Pineapple and Nut Cake

Makes one 20 cm/8 in cake

225 g/8 oz/1 cup caster (superfine) sugar

2 eggs

120 ml/4 fl oz/½ cup oil

1.5 ml/¼ tsp salt

5 ml/1 tsp bicarbonate of soda (baking soda)

100 g/4 oz/1 cup self-raising (self-rising) flour

5 ml/1 tsp ground cinnamon

175 g/6 oz carrots, grated

75 g/3 oz/¾ cup walnuts, chopped

225 g/8 oz crushed pineapple with its juice

For the icing (frosting):
15 g/½ oz/1 tbsp butter or margarine

50 g/2 oz/¼ cup cream cheese

10 ml/2 tsp lemon juice

Icing (confectioners') sugar, sifted

Line a large ring mould (tube pan) with baking parchment. Cream together the sugar, eggs and oil. Gently stir in the dry ingredients until well combined. Stir in the remaining cake ingredients. Pour the mixture into the prepared mould, stand it on a rack or upturned plate and microwave on High for 13 minutes or until just set. Leave to stand for 5 minutes, then turn out on to a rack to cool.

Meanwhile, make the icing. Put the butter or margarine, cream cheese and lemon juice in a bowl and microwave on High for 30–40 seconds. Gradually beat in enough icing sugar to make a thick consistency and beat until fluffy. When the cake is cold, spread over the icing.

Microwave Spiced Bran Cakes

Makes 15

75 g/3 oz/¾ cup All Bran cereal

250 ml/8 fl oz/1 cup milk

175 g/6 oz/1½ cups plain (all-purpose) flour

75 g/3 oz/1/3 cup caster (superfine) sugar

10 ml/2 tsp baking powder

10 ml/2 tsp ground mixed (apple-pie) spice

A pinch of salt

60 ml/4 tbsp golden (light corn) syrup

45 ml/3 tbsp oil

1 egg, lightly beaten

75 g/3 oz/½ cup raisins

15 ml/1 tbsp grated orange rind

Soak the cereal in the milk for 10 minutes. Mix together the flour, sugar, baking powder, mixed spice and salt, then mix into the cereal. Stir in the syrup, oil, egg, raisins and orange rind. Spoon into paper cases (cupcake papers) and microwave five cakes at a time on High for 4 minutes. Repeat for the remaining cakes.

Microwave Banana and Passion Fruit Cheesecake

Makes one 23 cm/9 in cake

100 g/4 oz/½ cup butter or margarine, melted

175 g/6 oz/1½ cups ginger biscuit (cookie) crumbs

250 g/9 oz/generous 1 cup cream cheese

175 ml/6 fl oz/¾ cup soured (dairy sour) cream

2 eggs, lightly beaten

100 g/4 oz/½ cup caster (superfine) sugar

Grated rind and juice of 1 lemon

150 ml/¼ pt/2/3 cup whipping cream

1 banana, sliced

1 passion fruit, chopped

Mix together the butter or margarine and biscuit crumbs and press into the base and sides of a 23 cm/9 in microwave flan dish. Microwave on High for 1 minute. Leave to cool.

> **Beat together the cream cheese and soured cream until smooth, then beat in the egg, sugar and lemon juice and rind. Spoon into the base and spread evenly. Cook on Medium for 8 minutes. Leave to cool.**

Whip the cream until stiff, then spread over the case. Top with banana slices and spoon the passion fruit flesh over the top.

Microwave Baked Orange Cheesecake

Makes one 20 cm/8 in cake

50 g/2 oz/¼ cup butter or margarine

12 digestive biscuits (Graham crackers), crushed

100 g/4 oz/½ cup caster (superfine) sugar

225 g/8 oz/1 cup cream cheese

2 eggs

30 ml/2 tbsp concentrated orange juice

15 ml/1 tbsp lemon juice

150 ml/¼ pt/2/3 cup soured (dairy sour) cream

A pinch of salt

1 orange

30 ml/2 tbsp apricot jam (conserve)

150 ml/¼ pt/2/3 cup double (heavy) cream

Melt the butter or margarine in a 20 cm/8 in microwave flan dish on High for 1 minute. Stir in the biscuit crumbs and 25 g/1 oz/2 tbsp of the sugar and press over the base and sides of the dish. Cream the cheese with the remaining sugar and the eggs, then stir in the orange and lemon juices, soured cream and salt. Spoon into the case (shell) and microwave on High for 2 minutes. Leave to stand for 2 minutes, then microwave on High for a further 2 minutes. Leave to stand for 1 minute, then microwave on High for 1 minute. Leave to cool.

Peel the orange and remove the segments from the membrane, using a sharp knife. Melt the jam and brush over the top of the cheesecake. Whip the cream and pipe round the edge of the cheesecake, then decorate with the orange segments.

Microwave Pineapple Cheesecake

Makes one 23 cm/9 in cake

100 g/4 oz/½ cup butter or margarine, melted

175 g/6 oz/1½ cups digestive biscuit (Graham cracker) crumbs

250 g/9 oz/generous 1 cup cream cheese

2 eggs, lightly beaten

5 ml/1 tsp grated lemon rind

30 ml/2 tbsp lemon juice

75 g/3 oz/1/3 cup caster (superfine) sugar

400 g/14 oz/1 large can pineapple, drained and crushed

150 ml/¼ pt/2/3 cup double (heavy) cream

Mix together the butter or margarine and biscuit crumbs and press into the base and sides of a 23 cm/9 in microwave flan dish. Microwave on High for 1 minute. Leave to cool.

> Beat together the cream cheese, eggs, lemon rind and juice and sugar until smooth. Stir in the pineapple and spoon into the base. Microwave on Medium for 6 minutes until firm. Leave to cool.

Whip the cream until stiff, then pile on top of the cheesecake.

Microwave Cherry and Nut Loaf

Makes one 900 g/2 lb loaf

175 g/6 oz/¾ cup butter or margarine, softened

175 g/6 oz/¾ cup soft brown sugar

3 eggs, beaten

225 g/8 oz/2 cups plain (all-purpose) flour

10 ml/2 tsp baking powder

A pinch of salt

45 ml/3 tbsp milk

75 g/3 oz/1/3 cup glacé (candied) cherries

75 g/3 oz/¾ cup chopped mixed nuts

25 g/1 oz/3 tbsp icing (confectioners') sugar, sifted

Cream together the butter or mar-garine and brown sugar until light and fluffy. Gradually beat in the eggs, then fold in the flour, baking powder and salt. Stir in enough of the milk to make a soft consistency, then stir in the cherries and nuts. Spoon into a greased and lined 900 g/2 lb microwave loaf dish and sprinkle with the sugar. Microwave on High for 7 minutes. Leave to stand for 5 minutes, then turn out on to a wire rack to finish cooling.

Microwave Chocolate Cake

Makes one 18 cm/7 in cake

225 g/8 oz/1 cup butter or margarine, softened

175 g/6 oz/¾ cup caster (superfine) sugar

150 g/5 oz/1¼ cups self-raising (self-rising) flour

50 g/2 oz/¼ cup cocoa (unsweetened chocolate) powder

5 ml/1 tsp baking powder

3 eggs, beaten

45 ml/3 tbsp milk

Mix together all the ingredients and spoon into a greased and lined 18 cm/7 in microwave dish. Microwave on High for 9 minutes until just firm to the touch. Leave to cool in the dish for 5 minutes, then turn out on to a wire rack to finish cooling.

Microwave Chocolate Almond Cake

Makes one 20 cm/8 in cake

For the cake:

100 g/4 oz/½ cup butter or margarine, softened

100 g/4 oz/½ cup caster (superfine) sugar

2 eggs, lightly beaten

100 g/4 oz/1 cup self-raising (self-rising) flour

50 g/2 oz/½ cup cocoa (unsweetened chocolate) powder

50 g/2 oz/½ cup ground almonds

150 ml/¼ pt/2/3 cup milk

60 ml/4 tbsp golden (light corn) syrup

For the icing (frosting):

100 g/4 oz/1 cup plain (semi-sweet) chocolate

25 g/1 oz/2 tbsp butter or margarine

8 whole almonds

To make the cake, cream together the butter or mar-garine and sugar until light and fluffy. Gradually beat in the eggs, then fold in the flour and cocoa, followed by the ground almonds. Stir in the milk and syrup and beat until light and soft. Spoon into a 20 cm/8 in microwave dish lined with clingfilm (plastic wrap) and microwave on High for 4 minutes. Remove from the oven, cover the top with foil and leave to cool slightly, then turn out on to a wire rack to finish cooling.

To make the icing, melt the chocolate and butter or margarine on High for 2 minutes. Beat well. Half-dip the almonds in the chocolate, then leave to set on a piece of greaseproof (waxed) paper. Pour the remaining icing over the cake and spread over the top and down the sides. Decorate with the almonds and leave to set.

Microwave Double Chocolate Brownies

Makes 8

150 g/5 oz/1¼ cups plain (semi-sweet) chocolate, coarsely chopped

75 g/3 oz/1/3 cup butter or margarine

175 g/6 oz/¾ cup soft brown sugar

2 eggs, lightly beaten

150 g/5 oz/1¼ cups plain (all-purpose) flour

2.5 ml/½ tsp baking powder

2.5 ml/½ tsp vanilla essence (extract)

30 ml/2 tbsp milk

Melt 50 g/2 oz/½ cup of the chocolate with the butter or margarine on High for 2 minutes. Beat in the sugar and eggs, then stir in the flour, baking powder, vanilla essence and milk until smooth. Spoon into a greased 20 cm/8 in square microwave dish and microwave on High for 7 minutes. Leave to cool in the dish for 10 minutes. Melt the remaining chocolate on High for 1 minute, then spread over the top of the cake and leave to cool. Cut into squares.

Microwave Chocolate Date Bars

Makes 8

50 g/2 oz/1/3 cup stoned (pitted) dates, chopped

60 ml/4 tbsp boiling water

65 g/2½ oz/1/3 cup butter or margarine, softened

225 g/8 oz/1 cup caster (superfine) sugar

1 egg

100 g/4 oz/1 cup plain (all-purpose) flour

10 ml/2 tsp cocoa (unsweetened chocolate) powder

2.5 ml/½ tsp baking powder

A pinch of salt

25 g/1 oz/¼ cup chopped mixed nuts

100 g/4 oz/1 cup plain (semi-sweet) chocolate, finely chopped

Mix the dates with the boiling water and leave to stand until cool. Cream together the butter or margarine with half the sugar until light and fluffy. Gradually work in the egg, then alternately fold in the flour, cocoa, baking powder and salt and the date mixture. Spoon into a greased and floured 20 cm/8 in square microwave dish. Mix the remaining sugar with the nuts and chocolate and sprinkle over the top, pressing down lightly. Microwave on High for 8 minutes. Leave to cool in the dish before cutting into squares.

Microwave Chocolate Squares

Makes 16

For the cake:

50 g/2 oz/¼ cup butter or margarine

5 ml/1 tsp caster (superfine) sugar

75 g/3 oz/¾ cup plain (all-purpose) flour

1 egg yolk

15 ml/1 tbsp water

175 g/6 oz/1½ cups plain (semi-sweet) chocolate, grated or finely chopped

For the topping:

50g /2 oz/¼ cup butter or margarine

50 g/2 oz/¼ cup caster (superfine) sugar

1 egg

2.5 ml/½ tsp vanilla essence (extract)

100 g/4 oz/1 cup walnuts, chopped

To make the cake, soften the butter or margarine and work in the sugar, flour, egg yolk and water. Spread the mixture evenly in a 20 cm/8 in square microwave dish and microwave on High for 2 minutes. Sprinkle over the chocolate and microwave on High for 1 minute. Spread evenly over the base and leave until hardened.

To make the topping, microwave the butter or margarine on High for 30 seconds. Stir in the remaining topping ingredients and spread over the chocolate. Microwave on High for 5 minutes. Leave to cool, then cut into squares.

Microwave Quick Coffee Cake

Makes one 19 cm/7 in cake

For the cake:

225 g/8 oz/1 cup butter or margarine, softened

225 g/8 oz/1 cup caster (superfine) sugar

225 g/8 oz/2 cups self-raising (self-rising) flour

5 eggs

45 ml/3 tbsp coffee essence (extract)

For the icing (frosting):

30 ml/2 tbsp coffee essence (extract)

175 g/6 oz/¾ cup butter or margarine

Icing (confectioners') sugar, sifted

Walnut halves to decorate

Mix together all the cake ingredients until well blended. Divided between two 19 cm/7 in microwave cake contain-ers and cook each one on high for 5–6 minutes. Remove from the microwave and leave to cool.

Blend together the icing ingredients, sweetening to taste with icing sugar. When cool, sandwich the cakes together with half the icing and spread the rest on top. Decorate with walnut halves.

Microwave Christmas Cake

Makes one 23 cm/9 in cake

150 g/5 oz/2/3 cup butter or margarine, softened

150 g/5 oz/2/3 cup soft brown sugar

3 eggs

30 ml/2 tbsp black treacle (molasses)

225 g/8 oz/2 cups self-raising (self-rising) flour

10 ml/2 tsp ground mixed (apple-pie) spice

2. 5 ml/½ tsp grated nutmeg

2.5 ml/½ tsp bicarbonate of soda (baking soda)

450 g/1 lb/22/3 cups mixed dried fruit (fruit cake mix)

50 g/2 oz/¼ cup glacé (candied) cherries

50 g/2 oz/1/3 cup chopped mixed peel

50 g/2 oz/½ cup chopped mixed nuts

30 ml/2 tbsp brandy

Additional brandy to mature the cake (optional)

Cream together the butter or margarine and sugar until light and fluffy. Gradually beat in the eggs and treacle, then fold in the flour, spices and bicarbonate of soda. Gently stir in the fruit, mixed peel and nuts, then stir in the brandy. Spoon into a base-lined 23 cm/9 in microwave dish and microwave on Low for 45–60 minutes. Leave to cool in the dish for 15 minutes before turning out on to a wire rack to finish cooling.

When cool, wrap the cake in foil and store in a cool, dark place for 2 weeks. If liked, pierce the top of the cake several times with a thin skewer and sprinkle over some additional brandy, then rewrap and store the cake. You can do this several times to create a richer cake.

Microwave Crumb Cake

Makes one 20 cm/8 in cake

300 g/10 oz/1¼ cups caster (superfine) sugar

225 g/8 oz/2 cups plain (all-purpose) flour

10 ml/2 tsp baking powder

5 ml/1 tsp ground cinnamon

100 g/4 oz/½ cup butter or margarine, softened

2 eggs, lightly beaten

100 ml/3½ fl oz/6½ tbsp milk

Mix together the sugar, flour, baking powder and cinnamon. Work in the butter or margarine, then set aside a quarter of the mixture. Mix together the eggs and milk and beat into the larger portion of cake mix. Spoon the mixture into a greased and floured 20 cm/8 in microwave dish and sprinkle with the reserved crumble mix. Microwave on High for 10 minutes. Leave to cool in the dish.

Microwave Date Bars

Makes 12

150 g/5 oz/1¼ cups self-raising (self-raising) flour

175 g/6 oz/¾ cup caster (superfine) sugar

100 g/4 oz/1 cup desiccated (shredded) coconut

100 g/4 oz/2/3 cups stoned (pitted) dates, chopped

50 g/2 oz/½ cup chopped mixed nuts

100 g/4 oz/½ cup butter or margarine, melted

1 egg, lightly beaten

Icing (confectioners') sugar for dusting

Mix together the dry ingredients. Stir in the butter or margarine and egg and mix to a firm dough. Press into the base of a 20 cm/8 in square microwave dish and microwave on Medium for 8 minutes until just firm. Leave in the dish for 10 minutes, then cut into bars and turn out on to a wire rack to finish cooling.

Microwave Fig Bread

Makes one 675 g/1½ lb loaf

100 g/4 oz/2 cups bran

50 g/2 oz/¼ cup soft brown sugar

45 ml/3 tbsp clear honey

100 g/4 oz/2/3 cup dried figs, chopped

50 g/2 oz/½ cup hazelnuts, chopped

300 ml/½ pt/1¼ cups milk

100 g/4 oz/1 cup wholemeal (wholewheat) flour

10 ml/2 tsp baking powder

A pinch of salt

Mix together all the ingredients to a stiff dough. Shape into a microwave loaf dish and level the surface. Cook on High for 7 minutes. Leave to cool in the dish for 10 minutes, then turn out on to a wire rack to finish cooling.

Microwave Flapjacks

Makes 24

175 g/6 oz/¾ cup butter or margarine, softened

50 g/2 oz/¼ cup caster (superfine) sugar

50 g/2 oz/¼ cup soft brown sugar

90 ml/6 tbsp golden (light corn) syrup

A pinch of salt

275 g/10 oz/2½ cups rolled oats

Mix together the butter or margarine and sugars in a large bowl and cook on High for 1 minute. Add the remaining ingredients and stir well. Spoon the mixture into a greased 18 cm/7 in microwave dish and press down lightly. Cook on High for 5 minutes. Leave to cool slightly, then cut into squares.

Microwave Fruit Cake

Makes one 18 cm/7 in cake

175 g/6 oz/¾ cup butter or margarine, softened

175 g/6 oz/¾ cup caster (superfine) sugar

Grated rind of 1 lemon

3 eggs, beaten

225 g/8 oz/2 cups plain (all-purpose) flour

5 ml/1 tsp ground mixed (apple-pie) spice

225 g/8 oz/1 1/3 cups raisins

225 g/8 oz/1 1/3 cups sultanas (golden raisins)

50 g/2 oz/¼ cup glacé (candied) cherries

50 g/2 oz/½ cup chopped mixed nuts

15 ml/1 tbsp golden (light corn) syrup

45 ml/3 tbsp brandy

Cream together the butter or mar-garine and sugar until light and fluffy. Mix in the lemon rind, then gradually beat in the eggs. Fold in the flour and mixed spice, then mix in the remaining ingredients. Spoon into a greased and lined 18 cm/7 in round microwave dish and microwave on Low for 35 minutes until a skewer inserted in the centre comes out clean. Leave to cool in the dish for 10 minutes, then turn out on to a wire rack to finish cooling.

Microwave Fruit and Coconut Squares

Makes 8

50 g/2 oz/¼ cup butter or margarine

9 digestive biscuits (Graham crackers), crushed

50 g/2 oz/½ cup desiccated (shredded) coconut

100 g/4 oz/2/3 cup chopped mixed (candied) peel

50 g/2 oz/1/3 cup stoned (pitted) dates, chopped

15 ml/1 tbsp plain (all-purpose) flour

25 g/1 oz/2 tbsp glacé (candied) cherries, chopped

100 g/4 oz/1 cup walnuts, chopped

150 ml/¼ pt/2/3 cup condensed milk

Melt the butter or margarine in a 20 cm/8 in square microwave dish on High for 40 seconds. Stir in the biscuit crumbs and spread evenly over the base of the dish. Sprinkle with the coconut, then with the mixed peel. Mix the dates with the flour, cherries and nuts and sprinkle over the top, then pour over the milk. Microwave on High for 8 minutes. Leave to cool in the dish, then cut into squares.

Microwave Fudge Cake

Makes one 20 cm/8 in cake

150 g/5 oz/1¼ cups plain (all-purpose) flour

5 ml/1 tsp baking powder

A pinch of bicarbonate of soda (baking soda)

A pinch of salt

300 g/10 oz/1¼ cups caster (superfine) sugar

50 g/2 oz/¼ cup butter or margarine, softened

250 ml/8 fl oz/1 cup milk

A few drops of vanilla essence (extract)

1 egg

100 g/4 oz /1 cup plain (semi-sweet) chocolate, chopped

50g /2 oz/½ cup chopped mixed nuts

Chocolate Butter Icing

Mix together the flour, baking powder, bicarbonate of soda and salt. Stir in the sugar, then beat in the butter or margarine, milk and vanilla essence until smooth. Beat in the egg. Microwave three-quarters of the chocolate on High for 2 minutes until melted, then beat into the cake mixture until creamy. Stir in the nuts. Spoon the mixture into two greased and floured 20 cm/8 in microwave dishes and microwave each one separately for 8 minutes. Remove from the oven, cover with foil and leave to cool for 10 minutes, then turn out on to a wire rack to finish cooling. Sandwich together with half the butter icing (frosting), then spread the remaining icing over the top and decorate with the reserved chocolate.

Microwave Gingerbread

Makes one 20 cm/8 in cake

50 g/2 oz/¼ cup butter or margarine

75 g/3 oz/¼ cup black treacle (molasses)

15 ml/1 tbsp caster (superfine) sugar

100 g/4 oz/1 cup plain (all-purpose) flour

5 ml/1 tsp ground ginger

2.5 ml/½ tsp ground mixed (apple-pie) spice

2.5 ml/½ tsp bicarbonate of soda (baking soda)

1 egg, beaten

Place the butter or margarine in a bowl and microwave on High for 30 seconds. Stir in the treacle and sugar and microwave on High for 1 minute. Stir in the flour, spices and bicarbonate of soda. Beat in the egg. Spoon the mixture into a greased 1.5 litre/2½ pint/6 cup dish and microwave on High for 4 minutes. Cool in the dish for 5 minutes, then turn out on to a wire rack to finish cooling.

Microwave Ginger Bars

Makes 12

For the cake:

150 g/5 oz/2/3 cup butter or margarine, softened

50 g/2 oz/¼ cup caster (superfine) sugar

100 g/4 oz/1 cup plain (all-purpose) flour

2.5 ml/½ tsp baking powder

5 ml/1 tsp ground ginger

For the topping:

15 g/½ oz/1 tbsp butter or margarine

15 ml/1 tbsp golden (light corn) syrup

A few drops of vanilla essence (extract)

5 ml/1 tsp ground ginger

50 g/2 oz/1/3 cup icing (confectioners') sugar

To make the cake, cream together the butter or mar-garine and sugar until light and fluffy. Stir in the flour, baking powder and ginger and mix to a smooth dough. Press into a 20 cm/8 in square microwave dish and microwave on Medium for 6 minutes until just firm.

To make the topping, melt the butter or margarine and syrup. Stir in the vanilla essence, ginger and icing sugar and whisk until thick. Spread evenly over the warm cake. Leave to cool in the dish, then cut into bars or squares.

Microwave Golden Cake

Makes one 20 cm/8 in cake

For the cake:

100 g/4 oz/½ cup butter or margarine, softened

100 g/4 oz/½ cup caster (superfine) sugar

2 eggs, lightly beaten

A few drops of vanilla essence (extract)

225 g/8 oz/2 cups plain (all-purpose) flour

10 ml/2 tsp baking powder

A pinch of salt

60 ml/4 tbsp milk

For the icing (frosting):

50 g/2 oz/¼ cup butter or margarine, softened

100 g/4 oz/2/3 cup icing (confectioner's) sugar

A few drops of vanilla essence (extract) (optional)

To make the cake, cream together the butter or margarine and sugar until light and fluffy. Gradually beat in the eggs, then fold in the flour, baking powder and salt. Stir in enough of the milk to give a soft, dropping consistency. Spoon into two greased and floured 20 cm/8 in microwave dishes and cook each cake separately on High for 6 minutes. Remove from the oven, cover with foil and leave to cool for 5 minutes, then turn out on to a wire rack to finish cooling.

To make the icing, beat the butter or margarine until soft, then beat in the icing sugar and vanilla essence, if liked. Sandwich the cakes together with half the icing, then spread the remainder over the top.

Microwave Honey and Hazelnut Cake

Makes one 18 cm/7 in cake

150 g/5 oz/2/3 cup butter or margarine, softened

100 g/4 oz/½ cup soft brown sugar

45 ml/3 tbsp clear honey

3 eggs, beaten

225 g/8 oz/2 cups self-raising (self-rising) flour

100 g/4 oz/1 cup ground hazelnuts

45 ml/3 tbsp milk

Butter Icing

Cream together the butter or margarine, sugar and honey until light and fluffy. Gradually beat in the eggs, then fold in the flour and hazelnuts and enough of the milk to give a soft consistency. Spoon into an 18 cm/7 in microwave dish and cook on Medium for 7 minutes. Leave to cool in the dish for 5 minutes, then turn out on to a wire rack to finish cooling. Cut the cake in half horizontally, then sandwich together with butter icing (frosting).

Microwave Chewy Muesli Bars

Makes about 10

100 g/4 oz/½ cup butter or margarine

175 g/6 oz/½ cup clear honey

50 g/2 oz/1/3 cup ready-to-eat dried apricots, chopped

50 g/2 oz/1/3 cup stoned (pitted) dates, chopped

75 g/3 oz/¾ cup chopped mixed nuts

100 g/4 oz/1 cup rolled oats

100 g/4 oz/½ cup soft brown sugar

1 egg, beaten

25 g/1 oz/2 tbsp self-raising (self-rising) flour

Place the butter or margarine and honey in a bowl and cook on High for 2 minutes. Mix in all the remaining ingredients. Spoon into a 20 cm/8 in microwave baking tray and microwave on High for 8 minutes. Leave to cool slightly, then cut into squares or slices.

Microwave Nut Cake

Makes one 20 cm/8 in cake

150 g/5 oz/1¼ cups plain (all-purpose) flour

A pinch of salt

5 ml/1 tsp ground cinnamon

75 g/3 oz/1/3 cup soft brown sugar

75 g/3 oz/1/3 cup caster (superfine) sugar

75 ml/5 tbsp oil

25 g/1 oz/¼ cup walnuts, chopped

5 ml/1 tsp baking powder

2.5 ml/½ tsp bicarbonate of soda (baking soda)

1 egg

150 ml/¼ pt/2/3 cup soured milk

Mix together the flour, salt and half the cinnamon. Stir in the sugars, then beat in the oil until well mixed. Remove 90 ml/6 tbsp of the mixture and stir it into the nuts and remaining cinnamon. Add the baking powder, bicarbonate of soda, egg and milk to the bulk of the mixture and beat until smooth. Spoon the main mixture into a greased and floured 20 cm/8 in microwave dish and sprinkle the nut mixture over the top. Microwave on High for 8 minutes. Leave to cool in the dish for 10 minutes and serve warm.

Microwave Orange Juice Cake

Makes one 20 cm/8 in cake

250 g/9 oz/2¼ cups plain (all-purpose) flour

225 g/8 oz/1 cup granulated sugar

15 ml/1 tbsp baking powder

2.5 ml/½ tsp salt

60 ml/4 tbsp oil

250 ml/8 fl oz/2 cups orange juice

2 eggs, separated

100 g/4 oz/½ cup caster (superfine) sugar

Orange Butter Icing

Orange Glacé Icing

Mix together the flour, granulated sugar, baking powder, salt, oil and half the orange juice and beat until well blended. Beat in the egg yolks and remaining orange juice until light and soft. Whisk the egg whites until stiff, then add half the caster sugar and beat until thick and glossy. Fold in the remaining sugar, then fold the egg whites into the cake mixture. Spoon into two greased and floured 20 cm/8 in microwave dishes and microwave each one separately on High for 6–8 minutes. Remove from the oven, cover with foil and leave to cool for 5 minutes, then turn out on to a wire rack to finish cooling. Sandwich the cakes together with orange butter icing (frosting) and spread the orange glacé icing over the top.

Microwave Pavlova

Makes one 23 cm/9 in cake

4 egg whites

225 g/8 oz/1 cup caster (superfine) sugar

2.5 ml/½ tsp vanilla essence (extract)

A few drops of wine vinegar

150 ml/¼ pt/2/3 cup whipping cream

1 kiwi fruit, sliced

100 g/4 oz strawberries, sliced

Beat the egg whites until they form soft peaks. Sprinkle in half the sugar and beat well. Gradually add the rest of the sugar, the vanilla essence and vinegar and beat until dissolved. Spoon the mixture into to a 23 cm/9 in circle on a piece of baking parchment. Microwave on High for 2 minutes. Leave to stand in the microwave with the door open for 10 minutes. Remove from the oven, tear off the backing paper and leave to cool. Whip the cream until stiff and spread over the top of the meringue. Arrange the fruit attractively on top.

Microwave Shortcake

Makes one 20 cm/8 in cake

225 g/8 oz/2 cups plain (all-purpose) flour

15 ml/1 tbsp baking powder

50 g/2 oz/¼ cup caster (superfine) sugar

100 g/4 oz/½ cup butter or margarine

75 ml/5 tbsp single (light) cream

1 egg

Mix together the flour, baking powder and sugar, then rub in the butter or margarine until the mixture resembles breadcrumbs. Mix together the cream and egg, then work into the flour mixture until you have a soft dough. Press into a greased 20 cm/8 in microwave dish and microwave on High for 6 minutes. Leave to stand for 4 minutes, then turn out and finish cooling on a wire rack.

Microwave Strawberry Shortcake

Makes one 20 cm/8 in cake

900 g/2 lb strawberries, thickly sliced

225 g/8 oz/1 cup caster (superfine) sugar

225 g/8 oz/2 cups plain (all-purpose) flour

15 ml/1 tbsp baking powder

175 g/6 oz/¾ cup butter or margarine

75 ml/5 tbsp single (light) cream

1 egg

150 ml/¼ pt/2/3 cup double (heavy) cream, whipped

Mix the strawberries with 175 g/ 6 oz/¾ cup of the sugar, then chill for at least 1 hour.

Mix together the flour, baking powder and remaining sugar, then rub in 100 g/ 4 oz/½ cup of the butter or margarine until the mixture resembles breadcrumbs. Mix together the single cream and egg, then work into the flour mixture until you have a soft dough. Press into a greased 20 cm/8 in microwave dish and microwave on High for 6 minutes. Leave to stand for 4 minutes, then turn out and split through the centre while still warm. Leave to cool.

Spread both cut surfaces with the remaining butter or margarine. Spread one-third of the whipped cream over the base, then cover with three-quarters of the strawberries. Top with a further one-third of the cream, then place the second shortcake on top. Top with the remaining cream and strawberries.

Microwave Sponge Cake

Makes one 18 cm/7 in cake

150 g/5 oz/1¼ cups self-raising (self-rising) flour

100 g/4 oz/½ cup butter or margarine

100 g/4 oz/½ cup caster (superfine) sugar

2 eggs

30 ml/2 tbsp milk

Beat together all the ingredients until smooth. Spoon into a base-lined 18 cm/7 in microwave dish and microwave on Medium for 6 minutes. Leave to cool in the dish for 5 minutes, then turn out on to a wire rack to finish cooling.

Microwave Sultana Bars

Makes 12

175 g/6 oz/¾ cup butter or margarine

100 g/4 oz/½ cup caster (superfine) sugar

15 ml/1 tbsp golden (light corn) syrup

75 g/3 oz/½ cup sultanas (golden raisins)

5 ml/1 tsp grated lemon rind

225 g/8 oz/2 cups self-raising (self-rising) flour

For the icing (frosting):
175 g/6 oz/1 cup icing (confectioners') sugar

30 ml/2 tbsp lemon juice

Microwave the butter or margarine, caster sugar and syrup on Medium for 2 minutes. Stir in the sultanas and lemon rind. Fold in the flour. Spoon into a greased and lined 20 cm/8 in square microwave dish and microwave on Medium for 8 minutes until just firm. Leave to cool slightly.

Place the icing sugar in a bowl and make a well in the centre. Gradually mix in the lemon juice to make a smooth icing. Spread over the cake while still just warm, then leave to cool completely.

Microwave Chocolate Biscuits

Makes 24

225 g/8 oz/1 cup butter or margarine, softened

100 g/4 oz/½ cup dark brown sugar

5 ml/1 tsp vanilla essence (extract)

225 g/8 oz/2 cups self-raising (self-rising) flour

50 g/2 oz/½ cup drinking chocolate powder

Cream together the butter, sugar and vanilla essence until light and fluffy. Gradually mix in the flour and chocolate and mix to a smooth dough. Shape into walnut-sized balls, arrange six at a time on a greased microwave baking (cookie) sheet and flatten slightly with a fork. Microwave each batch on High for 2 minutes, until all the biscuits (cookies) are cooked. Leave to cool on a wire rack.

Microwave Coconut Cookies

Makes 24

50 g/2 oz/¼ cup butter or margarine, softened

75 g/3 oz/1/3 cup caster (superfine) sugar

1 egg, lightly beaten

2.5 ml/½ tsp vanilla essence (extract)

75 g/3 oz/¾ cup plain (all-purpose) flour

25 g/1 oz/¼ cup desiccated (shredded) coconut

A pinch of salt

30 ml/2 tbsp strawberry jam (conserve)

Beat together the butter or margarine and sugar until light and fluffy. Stir in the egg and vanilla essence alternately with the flour, coconut and salt and mix to a smooth dough. Shape into walnut-sized balls and arrange six at a time on a greased microwave baking (cookie) sheet, then press lightly with a fork to flatten slightly. Microwave on High for 3 minutes until just firm. Transfer to a wire rack and place a spoonful of jam on the centre of each cookie. Repeat with the remaining cookies.

Microwave Florentines

Makes 12

50 g/2 oz/¼ cup butter or margarine

50 g/2 oz/¼ cup demerara sugar

15 ml/1 tbsp golden (light corn) syrup

50 g/2 oz/¼ cup glacé (candied) cherries

75 g/3 oz/¾ cup walnuts, chopped

25 g/1 oz/3 tbsp sultanas (golden raisins)

25 g/1 oz/¼ cup flaked (slivered) almonds

30 ml/2 tbsp chopped mixed (candied) peel

25 g/1 oz/¼ cup plain (all-purpose) flour

100 g/4 oz/1 cup plain (semi-sweet) chocolate, broken up (optional)

Microwave the butter or margarine, sugar and syrup on High for 1 minute until melted. Stir in the cherries, walnuts, sultanas and almonds, then mix in the mixed peel and flour. Place teaspoonfuls of the mixture, well apart, on greaseproof (waxed) paper and cook four at a time on High for 1½ minutes each batch. Neaten the edges with a knife, leave to cool on the paper for 3 minutes, then transfer to a wire rack to finish cooling. Repeat with the remaining biscuits. If liked, melt the chocolate in a bowl for 30 seconds and spread over one side of the florentines, then leave to set.

Microwave Hazelnut and Cherry Biscuits

Makes 24

100 g/4 oz/½ cup butter or margarine, softened

100 g/4 oz/½ cup caster (superfine) sugar

1 egg, beaten

175 g/6 oz/1½ cups plain (all-purpose) flour

50 g/2 oz/½ cup ground hazelnuts

100 g/4 oz/½ cup glacé (candied) cherries

Cream together the butter or margarine and sugar until light and fluffy. Gradually beat in the egg, then fold in the flour, hazelnuts and cherries. Place spoonfuls well spaced out on microwave baking (cookie) sheets and microwave eight biscuits (cookies) at a time on High for about 2 minutes until just firm.

Microwave Sultana Biscuits

Makes 24

225 g/8 oz/2 cups plain (all-purpose) flour

5 ml/1 tsp ground mixed (apple-pie) spice

175 g/6 oz/¾ cup butter or margarine, softened

100 g/4 oz/2/3 cup sultanas (golden raisins)

175 g/6 oz/¾ cup demerara sugar

Mix together the flour and mixed spice, then blend in the butter or margarine, sultanas and 100 g/4 oz/½ cup of the sugar to make a soft dough. Roll into two sausage shapes about 18 cm/7 in long and roll in the remaining sugar. Cut into slices and arrange six at a time on a greased microwave baking (cookie) sheet and microwave on High for 2 minutes. Leave to cool on a wire rack and repeat with the remaining biscuits (cookies).

Microwave Banana Bread

Makes one 450 g/1 lb loaf

75 g/3 oz/1/3 cup butter or margarine, softened

175 g/6 oz/¾ cup caster (superfine) sugar

2 eggs, lightly beaten

200 g/7 oz/1¾ cups plain (all-purpose) flour

10 ml/2 tsp baking powder

2.5 ml/½ tsp bicarbonate of soda (baking soda)

A pinch of salt

2 ripe bananas

15 ml/1 tbsp lemon juice

60 ml/4 tbsp milk

50 g/2 oz/½ cup walnuts, chopped

Cream together the butter or margarine and sugar until light and fluffy. Gradually beat in the eggs, then fold in the flour, baking powder, bicarbonate of soda and salt. Mash the bananas with the lemon juice, then fold into the mixture with the milk and walnuts. Spoon into a greased and floured 450 g/1 lb microwave loaf tin (pan) and microwave on High for 12 minutes. Remove from the oven, cover with foil and leave to cool for 10 minutes, then turn out on to a wire rack to finish cooling.

Microwave Cheese Bread

Makes one 450 g/1 lb loaf

50 g/2 oz/¼ cup butter or margarine

250 ml/8 fl oz/1 cup milk

2 eggs, lightly beaten

225 g/8 oz/2 cups plain (all-purpose) flour

10 ml/2 tsp baking powder

10 ml/2 tsp mustard powder

2.5 ml/½ tsp salt

175 g/6 oz/1½ cups Cheddar cheese, grated

Melt the butter or margarine in a small bowl on High for 1 minute. Stir in the milk and eggs. Mix together the flour, baking powder, mustard, salt and 100 g/4 oz/1 cup of the cheese. Stir in the milk mixture until well blended. Spoon into a microwave loaf tin (pan) and microwave on High for 9 minutes. Sprinkle with the remaining cheese, cover with foil and leave to stand for 20 minutes.

Microwave Walnut Loaf

Makes one 450 g/1 lb loaf

225 g/8 oz/2 cups plain (all-purpose) flour

300 g/10 oz/1¼ cups caster (superfine) sugar

5 ml/1 tsp baking powder

A pinch of salt

100 g/4 oz/½ cup butter or margarine, softened

150 ml/¼ pt/2/3 cup milk

2.5 ml/½ tsp vanilla essence (extract)

4 egg whites

50 g/2 oz/½ cup walnuts, chopped

Mix together the flour, sugar, baking powder and salt. Beat in the butter or margarine, then the milk and vanilla essence. Beat in the egg whites until creamy, then fold in the nuts. Spoon into a greased and floured 450 g/1 lb microwave loaf tin (pan) and microwave on High for 12 minutes. Remove from the oven, cover with foil and leave to cool for 10 minutes, then turn out on to a wire rack to finish cooling.

No-bake Amaretti Cake

Makes one 20 cm/8 in cake

100 g/4 oz/½ cup butter or margarine

175 g/6 oz/1½ cups plain (semi-sweet) chocolate

75 g/3 oz Amaretti biscuits (cookies), coarsely crushed

175 g/6 oz/1½ cups walnuts, chopped

50 g/2 oz/½ cup pine nuts

75 g/3 oz/1/3 cup glacé (candied) cherries, chopped

30 ml/2 tbsp Grand Marnier

225 g/8 oz/1 cup Mascarpone cheese

Melt the butter or margarine and chocolate in a heatproof bowl set over a pan of gently simmering water. Remove from the heat and stir in the biscuits, nuts and cherries. Spoon into a sandwich tin (pan) lined with clingfilm (plastic wrap) and press down gently. Chill for 1 hour until set. Turn out on to a serving plate and remove the clingfilm. Beat the Grand Marnier into the Mascarpone and spoon over the base.

American Crispy Rice Bars

Makes about 24 bars

50 g/2 oz/¼ cup butter or margarine

225 g/8 oz white marshmallows

5 ml/1 tsp vanilla essence (extract)

150 g/5 oz/5 cups puffed rice cereal

Melt the butter or margarine in a large pan over a low heat. Add the marshmallows and cook, stirring continuously, until the marshmallows have melted and the mixture is syrupy. Remove from the heat and add the vanilla essence. Stir in the rice cereal until evenly coated. Press into a 23 cm/9 in square tin (pan) and cut into bars. Leave to set.

Apricot Squares

Makes 12

50 g/2 oz/¼ cup butter or margarine

175 g/6 oz/1 small can evaporated milk

15 ml/1 tbsp clear honey

45 ml/3 tbsp apple juice

50 g/2 oz/¼ cup soft brown sugar

50 g/2 oz/1/3 cup sultanas (golden raisins)

225 g/8 oz/11/3 cups ready-to-eat dried apricots, chopped

100 g/4 oz/1 cup desiccated (shredded) coconut

225 g/8 oz/2 cups rolled oats

Melt the butter or margarine with the milk, honey, apple juice and sugar. Stir in the remaining ingredients. Press into a greased 25 cm/12 in baking tin (pan) and chill before cutting into squares.

Apricot Swiss Roll Cake

Makes one 23 cm/9 in cake

400 g/14 oz/1 large can apricot halves, drained and juice reserved

50 g/2 oz/½ cup custard powder

75 g/3 oz/¼ cup apricot jelly (clear conserve)

75 g/3 oz/½ cup ready-to-eat dried apricots, chopped

400 g/14 oz/1 large can condensed milk

225 g/8 oz/1 cup cottage cheese

45 ml/3 tbsp lemon juice

1 Swiss Roll, sliced

Make up the apricot juice with water to make 500 ml/17 fl oz/2¼ cups. Mix the custard powder to a paste with a little of the liquid, then bring the remainder to the boil. Stir in the custard paste and apricot jelly and simmer until thick and shiny, stirring continuously. Mash the canned apricots and add to the mixture with the dried apricots. Leave to cool, stirring occasionally.

Beat together the condensed milk, cottage cheese and lemon juice until well blended, then stir into the jelly mixture. Line a 23 cm/9 in cake tin (pan) with clingfilm (plastic wrap) and arrange the Swiss (jelly) roll slices over the base and sides of the tin. Spoon in the cake mixture and chill until set. Turn out carefully when ready to serve.

Broken Biscuit Cakes

Makes 12

100 g/4 oz/½ cup butter or margarine

30 ml/2 tbsp caster (superfine) sugar

15 ml/1 tbsp golden (light corn) syrup

30 ml/2 tbsp cocoa (unsweetened chocolate) powder

225 g/8 oz/2 cups broken biscuit (cookie) crumbs

50 g/2 oz/1/3 cup sultanas (golden raisins)

Melt the butter or margarine with the sugar and syrup without allowing the mixture to boil. Stir in the cocoa, biscuits and sultanas. Press into a greased 25 cm/10 in baking tin (pan), leave to cool, then chill until firm. Cut into squares.

No-bake Buttermilk Cake

Makes one 23 cm/9 in cake

30 ml/2 tbsp custard powder

100 g/4 oz/½ cup caster (superfine) sugar

450 ml/¾ pt/2 cups milk

175 ml/6 fl oz/¾ cup buttermilk

25 g/1 oz/2 tbsp butter or margarine

400 g/12 oz plain biscuits (cookies), crushed

120 ml/4 fl oz/½ cup whipping cream

Blend the custard powder and sugar to a paste with a little of the milk. Bring the remaining milk to the boil. Stir it into the paste, then return the whole mixture to the pan and stir over a low heat for about 5 minutes until thickened. Stir in the buttermilk and butter or margarine. Spoon layers of crushed biscuits and custard mixture into a 23 cm/9 in cake tin (pan) lined with clingfilm (plastic wrap), or into a glass dish. Press down gently and chill until set. Whip the cream until stiff, then pipe rosettes of cream on the top of the cake. Either serve from the dish, or lift out carefully to serve.

Chestnut Slice

Makes one 900 g/2 lb loaf

225 g/8 oz/2 cups plain (semi-sweet) chocolate

100 g/4 oz/½ cup butter or margarine, softened

100 g/4 oz/½ cup caster (superfine) sugar

450 g/1 lb/1 large can unsweetened chestnut purée

25 g/1 oz/¼ cup rice flour

A few drops of vanilla essence (extract)

150 ml/¼ pt/2/3 cup whipping cream, whipped

Grated chocolate to decorate

Melt the plain chocolate in a heatproof bowl over a pan of gently simmering water. Cream together the butter or margarine and sugar until light and fluffy. Beat in the chestnut purée, chocolate, rice flour and vanilla essence. Turn into a greased and lined 900 g/2 lb loaf tin (pan) and chill until firm. Decorate with whipped cream and grated chocolate before serving.

Chestnut Sponge Cake

Makes one 900 g/2 lb cake

For the cake:
400 g/14 oz/1 large can sweetened chestnut purée

100 g/4 oz/½ cup butter or margarine, softened

1 egg

A few drops of vanilla essence (extract)

30 ml/2 tbsp brandy

24 sponge finger biscuits (cookies)

For the glaze:

30 ml/2 tbsp cocoa (unsweetened chocolate) powder

15 ml/1 tbsp caster (superfine) sugar

30 ml/2 tbsp water

For the butter cream:
100 g/4 oz/½ cup butter or margarine, softened

100 g/4 oz/2/3 cup icing (confectioners') sugar, sifted

15 ml/1 tbsp coffee essence (extract)

To make the cake, blend together the chestnut purée, butter or margarine, egg, vanilla essence and 15 ml/1 tbsp of the brandy and beat until smooth. Grease and line a 900 g/2 lb loaf tin (pan) and line the base and sides with the sponge fingers. Sprinkle the remaining brandy over the biscuits and spoon the chestnut mixture into the centre. Chill until firm.

Lift out of the tin and remove the lining paper. Dissolve the glaze ingredients in a heatproof bowl set over a pan of gently simmering water, stirring until smooth. Leave to cool slightly, then brush most of the glaze over the top of the cake. Cream together the butter cream ingredients until smooth, then pipe into swirls around the edge of the cake. Drizzle with the reserved glaze to finish.

Chocolate and Almond Bars

Makes 12

175 g/6 oz/1½ cups plain (semi-sweet) chocolate, chopped

3 eggs, separated

120 ml/4 fl oz/½ cup milk

10 ml/2 tsp powdered gelatine

120 ml/4 fl oz/½ cup double (heavy) cream

45 ml/3 tbsp caster (superfine) sugar

60 ml/4 tbsp flaked (slivered) almonds, toasted

Melt the chocolate in a heatproof bowl set over a pan of gently simmering water. Remove from the heat and beat in the egg yolks. Boil the milk in a separate pan, then whisk in the gelatine. Stir into the chocolate mixture, then stir in the cream. Beat the egg whites until stiff, then add the sugar and beat again until stiff and glossy. Fold into the mixture. Spoon into a greased and lined 450 g/1 lb loaf tin (pan), sprinkle with the toasted almonds and leave to cool, then chill for at least 3 hours until set. Turn over and cut into thick slices to serve

Chocolate Crisp Cake

Makes one 450 g/1 lb loaf

150 g/5 oz/2/3 cup butter or margarine

30 ml/2 tbsp golden (light corn) syrup

175 g/6 oz/1½ cups digestive biscuit (Graham cracker) crumbs

50 g/2 oz/2 cups puffed rice cereal

25 g/1 oz/3 tbsp sultanas (golden raisins)

25 g/1 oz/2 tbsp glacé (candied) cherries, chopped

225 g/8 oz/2 cups chocolate chips

30 ml/2 tbsp water

175 g/6 oz/1 cup icing (confectioners') sugar, sifted

Melt 100 g/4 oz/½ cup of the butter or margarine with the syrup, then remove from the heat and stir in the biscuit crumbs, cereal, sultanas, cherries and three-quarters of the chocolate chips. Spoon into a greased and lined 450 g/1 lb loaf tin (pan) and smooth the top. Chill until firm. Melt the remaining butter or margarine with the remaining chocolate and the water. Stir in the icing sugar and mix until smooth. Remove the cake from the tin and halve lengthways. Sandwich together with half the chocolate icing (frosting), place on a serving plate, then pour over the remaining icing. Chill before serving.

Chocolate Crumb Squares

Makes about 24

225 g/8 oz digestive biscuits (Graham crackers)

100 g/4 oz/½ cup butter or margarine

25 g/1 oz/2 tbsp caster (superfine) sugar

15 ml/1 tbsp golden (light corn) syrup

45 ml/3 tbsp cocoa (unsweetened chocolate) powder

200 g/7 oz/1¾ cups chocolate cake covering

Place the biscuits in a plastic bag and crush with a rolling pin. Melt the butter or margarine in a pan, then stir in the sugar and syrup. Remove from the heat and stir in the biscuit crumbs and cocoa. Turn into a greased and lined 18 cm/7 in square cake tin and press down evenly. Leave to cool, then chill in the fridge until set.

Melt the chocolate in a heatproof bowl set over a pan of gently simmering water. Spread over the biscuit, marking into lines with a fork while setting. Cut into squares when firm.

Chocolate Fridge Cake

Makes one 450 g/1 lb cake

100 g/4 oz/½ cup soft brown sugar

100 g/4 oz/½ cup butter or margarine

50 g/2 oz/½ cup drinking chocolate powder

25 g/1 oz/¼ cup cocoa (unsweetened chocolate) powder

30 ml/2 tbsp golden (light corn) syrup

150 g/5 oz digestive biscuits (Graham crackers) or rich tea biscuits

50 g/2 oz/¼ cup glacé (candied) cherries or mixed nuts and raisins

100 g/4 oz/1 cup milk chocolate

Place the sugar, butter or margarine, drinking chocolate, cocoa and syrup in a pan and warm gently until the butter has melted, stirring well. Remove from the heat and crumble in the biscuits. Stir in the cherries or nuts and raisins and spoon into a 450 g/1 lb loaf tin (pan). Leave in the fridge to cool.

Melt the chocolate in a heatproof bowl over a pan of gently simmering water. Spread over the top of the cooled cake and slice when set.

Chocolate and Fruit Cake

Makes one 18 cm/7 in cake

100 g/4 oz/½ cup butter or margarine, melted

100 g/4 oz/½ cup soft brown sugar

225 g/8 oz/2 cups digestive biscuit (Graham cracker) crumbs

50 g/2 oz/1/3 cup sultanas (golden raisins)

45 ml/3 tbsp cocoa (unsweetened chocolate) powder

1 egg, beaten

A few drops of vanilla essence (extract)

Mix the butter or margarine and sugar, then stir in the remaining ingredients and beat well. Spoon into a greased 18 cm/7 in sandwich tin (pan) and smooth the surface. Chill until set.

Chocolate and Ginger Squares

Makes 24

100 g/4 oz/½ cup butter or margarine

100 g/4 oz/½ cup soft brown sugar

30 ml/2 tbsp cocoa (unsweetened chocolate) powder

1 egg, lightly beaten

225 g/8 oz/2 cups ginger biscuit (cookie) crumbs

15 ml/1 tbsp chopped crystallised (candied) ginger

Melt the butter or margarine, then stir in the sugar and cocoa until well blended. Mix in the egg, biscuit crumbs and ginger. Press into a Swiss roll tin (jelly roll pan) and chill until firm. Cut into squares.

Luxury Chocolate and Ginger Squares

Makes 24

100 g/4 oz/½ cup butter or margarine

100 g/4 oz/½ cup soft brown sugar

30 ml/2 tbsp cocoa (unsweetened chocolate) powder

1 egg, lightly beaten

225 g/8 oz/2 cups ginger biscuit (cookie) crumbs

15 ml/1 tbsp chopped crystallised (candied) ginger

100 g/4 oz/1 cup plain (semi-sweet) chocolate

Melt the butter or margarine, then stir in the sugar and cocoa until well blended. Mix in the egg, biscuit crumbs and ginger. Press into a Swiss roll tin (jelly roll pan) and chill until firm.

> Melt the chocolate in a heatproof bowl set over a pan of gently simmering water. Spread over the cake and leave to set. Cut into squares when the chocolate is almost hard.

Honey Chocolate Cookies

Makes 12

225 g/8 oz/1 cup butter or margarine

30 ml/2 tbsp clear honey

90 ml/6 tbsp carob or cocoa (unsweetened chocolate) powder

225 g/8 oz/2 cups sweet biscuit (cookie) crumbs

Melt the butter or margarine, honey and carob or cocoa powder in a pan until well blended. Mix in the biscuit crumbs. Spoon into a greased 20 cm/8 in square cake tin (pan) and leave to cool, then cut into squares.

Chocolate Layer Cake

Makes one 450 g/1 lb cake

300 ml/½ pt/1¼ cups double (heavy) cream

225 g/8 oz/2 cups plain (semi-sweet) chocolate, broken up

5 ml/1 tsp vanilla essence (extract)

20 plain biscuits (cookies)

Heat the cream in a pan over a low heat until almost boiling. Remove from the heat and add the chocolate, stir, cover and leave for 5 minutes. Stir in the vanilla essence and mix until well blended, then chill until the mixture begins to thicken.

Line a 450g /1 lb loaf tin (pan) with clingfilm (plastic wrap). Spread a layer of chocolate on the bottom, then arrange a few biscuits in a layer on top. Continue layering the chocolate and biscuits until you have used them up. Finish with a layer of chocolate. Cover with clingfilm and chill for at least 3 hours. Turn out the cake and remove the clingfilm.

Nice Chocolate Bars

Makes 12

100 g/4 oz/½ cup butter or margarine

30 ml/2 tbsp golden (light corn) syrup

30 ml/2 tbsp cocoa (unsweetened chocolate) powder

225 g/8 oz/1 packet Nice or plain biscuits (cookies), roughly crushed

100 g/4 oz/1 cup plain (semi-sweet) chocolate, diced

Melt the butter or margarine and syrup, then remove from the heat and stir in the cocoa and crushed biscuits. Spread the mixture in a 23 cm/9 in square cake tin (pan) and level the surface. Melt the chocolate in a heatproof bowl over a pan of gently simmering water and spread over the top. Leave to cool slightly, then cut into bars or squares and chill until set.

Chocolate Praline Squares

Makes 12

100 g/4 oz/½ cup butter or margarine

30 ml/2 tbsp caster (superfine) sugar

15 ml/1 tbsp golden (light corn) syrup

15 ml/1 tbsp drinking chocolate powder

225 g/8 oz digestive biscuits (Graham crackers), crushed

200 g/7 oz/1¾ cups plain (semi-sweet) chocolate

100 g/4 oz/1 cup chopped mixed nuts

Melt the butter or margarine, sugar, syrup and drinking chocolate in a pan. Bring to the boil, then boil for 40 seconds. Remove from the heat and stir in the biscuits and nuts. Press into a greased 28 x 18 cm/11 x 7 in cake tin (pan). Melt the chocolate in a heatproof bowl over a pan of gently simmering water. Spread over the biscuits and leave to cool, then chill for 2 hours before cutting into squares.

Coconut Crunchies

Makes 12

100 g/4 oz/1 cup plain (semi-sweet) chocolate

30 ml/2 tbsp milk

30 ml/2 tbsp golden (light corn) syrup

100 g/4 oz/4 cups puffed rice cereal

50 g/2 oz/½ cup desiccated (shredded) coconut

Melt the chocolate, milk and syrup in a pan. Remove from the heat and stir in the cereal and coconut. Spoon into paper cake cases (cupcake papers) and leave to set.

Crunch Bars

Makes 12

175 g/6 oz/¾ cup butter or margarine

50 g/2 oz/¼ cup soft brown sugar

30 ml/2 tbsp golden (light corn) syrup

45 ml/3 tbsp cocoa (unsweetened chocolate) powder

75 g/3 oz/½ cup raisins or sultanas (golden raisins)

350 g/12 oz/3 cups oat crunch cereal

225 g/8 oz/2 cups plain (semi-sweet) chocolate

Melt the butter or margarine with the sugar, syrup and cocoa. Stir in the raisins or sultanas and the cereal. Press the mixture into a greased 25 cm/12 in baking tin (pan). Melt the chocolate in a heatproof bowl over a pan of gently simmering water. Spread over the bars and leave to cool, then chill before cutting into bars.

Coconut and Raisin Crunchies

Makes 12

100 g/4 oz/1 cup white chocolate

30 ml/2 tbsp milk

30 ml/2 tbsp golden (light corn) syrup

175 g/6 oz/6 cups puffed rice cereal

50 g/2 oz/1/3 cup raisins

Melt the chocolate, milk and syrup in a pan. Remove from the heat and stir in the cereal and raisins. Spoon into paper cake cases (cupcake papers) and leave to set.

Coffee Milk Squares

Makes 20

25 g/1 oz/2 tbsp powdered gelatine

75 ml/5 tbsp cold water

225 g/8 oz/2 cups plain biscuit (cookie) crumbs

50 g/2 oz/¼ cup butter or margarine, melted

400 g/14 oz/1 large can evaporated milk

150 g/5 oz/2/3 cup caster (superfine) sugar

400 ml/14 fl oz/1¾ cups strong black coffee, ice cold

Whipped cream and crystallised (candied) orange slices to decorate

Sprinkle the gelatine over the water in a bowl and leave until spongy. Stand the bowl in a pan of hot water and leave until dissolved. Leave to cool slightly. Stir the biscuit crumbs into the melted butter and press into the base and sides of a greased 30 x 20 cm/12 x 8 in rectangular cake tin (pan). Beat the evaporated milk until thick, then gradually beat in the sugar, followed by the dissolved gelatine and the coffee. Spoon over the base and chill until set. Cut into squares and decorate with piped whipped cream and crystallised (candied) orange slices.

No-bake Fruit Cake

Makes one 23 cm/9 in cake

450 g/1 lb/22/3 cups dried mixed fruit (fruit cake mix)

450 g/1 lb plain biscuits (cookies), crushed

100 g/4 oz/½ cup butter or margarine, melted

100 g/4 oz/½ cup soft brown sugar

400 g/14 oz/1 large can condensed milk

5 ml/1 tsp vanilla essence (extract)

Mix together all the ingredients until well blended. Spoon into a greased 23 cm/9 in cake tin (pan) lined with clingfilm (plastic wrap) and press down. Chill until firm.

Fruity Squares

Makes about 12

100 g/4 oz/½ cup butter or margarine

100 g/4 oz/½ cup soft brown sugar

400 g/14 oz/1 large can condensed milk

5 ml/1 tsp vanilla essence (extract)

250 g/9 oz/1½ cups dried mixed fruit (fruit cake mix)

100 g/4 oz/½ cup glacé (candied) cherries

50 g/2 oz/½ cup chopped mixed nuts

400 g/14 oz plain biscuits (cookies), crushed

Melt the butter or margarine and sugar over a low heat. Stir in the condensed milk and vanilla essence and remove from the heat. Mix in the remaining ingredients. Press into a greased Swiss roll tin (jelly roll pan) and chill for 24 hours until firm. Cut into squares.

Fruit and Fibre Crackles

Makes 12

100 g/4 oz/1 cup plain (semi-sweet) chocolate

50 g/2 oz/¼ cup butter or margarine

15 ml/1 tbsp golden (light corn) syrup

100 g/4 oz/1 cup fruit and fibre breakfast cereal

Melt the chocolate in a heatproof bowl over a pan of gently simmering water. Beat in the butter or margarine and syrup. Stir in the cereal. Spoon into paper cake cases (cupcake papers) and leave to cool and set.

Nougat Layer Cake

Makes one 900 g/2 lb cake

15 g/½ oz/1 tbsp powdered gelatine

100 ml/3½ fl oz/6½ tbsp water

1 packet trifle sponges

225 g/8 oz/1 cup butter or margarine, softened

50 g/2 oz/¼ cup caster (superfine) sugar

400 g/14 oz/1 large can condensed milk

5 ml/1 tsp lemon juice

5 ml/1 tsp vanilla essence (extract)

5 ml/1 tsp cream of tartar

100 g/4 oz/2/3 cup dried mixed fruit (fruit cake mix), chopped

Sprinkle the gelatine over the water in a small bowl, then stand the bowl in a pan of hot water until the gelatine is transparent. Cool slightly. Line a 900 g/2 lb loaf tin (pan) with foil so that the foil will cover the top of the tin, then arrange half the trifle sponges on the base. Beat together the butter or margarine and sugar until creamy, then beat in all the remaining ingredients. Spoon into the tin and arrange the remaining trifle sponges on top. Cover with foil and put a weight on the top. Chill until firm.

Milk and Nutmeg Squares

Makes 20

For the base:

225 g/8 oz/2 cups plain biscuit (cookie) crumbs

30 ml/2 tbsp soft brown sugar

2.5 ml/½ tsp grated nutmeg

100 g/4 oz/½ cup butter or margarine, melted

For the filling:

1.2 litres/2 pts/5 cups milk

25 g/1 oz/2 tbsp butter or margarine

2 eggs, separated

225 g/8 oz/1 cup caster (superfine) sugar

100 g/4 oz/1 cup cornflour (cornstarch)

50 g/2 oz/½ cup plain (all-purpose) flour

5 ml/1 tsp baking powder

A pinch of grated nutmeg

Grated nutmeg for sprinkling

To make the base, mix the biscuit crumbs, sugar and nutmeg into the melted butter or margarine and press into the base of a greased 30 x 20 cm/12 x 8 in cake tin (pan).

To make the filling, bring 1 litre/ 1¾ pts/4¼ cups of the milk to the boil in a large pan. Add the butter or margarine. Beat the egg yolks with the remaining milk. Mix in the sugar, cornflour, flour, baking powder and nutmeg. Beat a little of the boiling milk into the egg yolk mixture until blended to a paste, then mix the paste into the boiling milk, stirring continuously over a low heat for a few minutes until thickened. Remove from the heat. Beat the egg whites until stiff, then fold them into the mixture. Spoon over the base and sprinkle generously with nutmeg. Leave to cool, then chill and cut into squares before serving.

Muesli Crunch

Makes about 16 squares

400 g/14 oz/3½ cups plain (semi-sweet) chocolate

45 ml/3 tbsp golden (light corn) syrup

25 g/1 oz/2 tbsp butter or margarine

About 225 g/8 oz/2/3 cup muesli

Melt together half the chocolate, the syrup and butter or margarine. Gradually stir in enough muesli to make a stiff mixture. Press into a greased Swiss roll tin (jelly roll pan). Melt the remaining chocolate and smooth over the top. Chill in the fridge before cutting into squares.

Orange Mousse Squares

Makes 20

25 g/1 oz/2 tbsp powdered gelatine

75 ml/5 tbsp cold water

225 g/8 oz/2 cups plain biscuit (cookie) crumbs

50 g/2 oz/¼ cup butter or margarine, melted

400 g/14 oz/1 large can evaporated milk

150 g/5 oz/2/3 cup caster (superfine) sugar

400 ml/14 fl oz/1¾ cups orange juice

Whipped cream and chocolate sweets to decorate

Sprinkle the gelatine over the water in a bowl and leave until spongy. Stand the bowl in a pan of hot water and leave until dissolved. Leave to cool slightly. Stir the biscuit crumbs into the melted butter and press on to the base and sides of a greased 30 x 20 cm/12 x 8 in shallow cake tin (pan). Beat the milk until thick, then gradually beat in the sugar, followed by the dissolved gelatine and the orange juice. Spoon over the base and chill until set. Cut into squares and decorate with piped whipped cream and chocolate sweets.

Peanut Squares

Makes 18

225 g/8 oz/2 cups plain biscuit (cookie) crumbs

100 g/4 oz/½ cup butter or margarine, melted

225 g/8 oz/1 cup crunchy peanut butter

25 g/1 oz/2 tbsp glacé (candied) cherries

25 g/1 oz/3 tbsp currants

Mix together all the ingredients until well blended. Press into a greased 25 cm/12 in baking tin (pan) and chill until firm, then cut into squares.

Peppermint Caramel Cakes

Makes 16

400 g/14 oz/1 large can condensed milk

600 ml/1 pt/2½ cups milk

30 ml/2 tbsp custard powder

225 g/8 oz/2 cups digestive biscuit (Graham cracker) crumbs

100 g/4 oz/1 cup peppermint chocolate, broken into pieces

Place the unopened can of condensed milk in a pan filled with sufficient water to cover the can. Bring to the boil, cover and simmer for 3 hours, topping up with boiling water as necessary. Leave to cool, then open the can and remove the caramel.

Heat 500 ml/17 fl oz/2¼ cups of the milk with the caramel, bring to the boil and stir together until melted. Mix the custard powder to a paste with the remaining milk, then stir it into the pan and continue to simmer until thickened, stirring continuously. Sprinkle half the biscuit crumbs over the base of a greased 20 cm/8 in square cake tin (pan), then spoon half the caramel custard on top and sprinkle with half the chocolate. Repeat the layers, then leave to cool. Chill, then cut into portions to serve.

Rice Cookies

Makes 24

175 g/6 oz/½ cup clear honey

225 g/8 oz/1 cup granulated sugar

60 ml/4 tbsp water

350 g/12 oz/1 box puffed rice cereal

100 g/4 oz/1 cup roasted peanuts

Melt the honey, sugar and water in a large pan, then leave to cool for 5 minutes. Stir in the cereal and peanuts. Roll into balls, place in paper cake cases (cupcake papers) and leave until cool and set.

Rice and Chocolate Toffette

Makes 225 g/8 oz

50 g/2 oz/¼ cup butter or margarine

30 ml/2 tbsp golden (light corn) syrup

30 ml/2 tbsp cocoa (unsweetened chocolate) powder

60 ml/4 tbsp caster (superfine) sugar

50 g/2 oz/½ cup ground rice

Melt the butter and syrup. Stir in the cocoa and sugar until dissolved, then stir in the ground rice. Bring gently to the boil, reduce the heat and simmer gently for 5 minutes, stirring continuously. Spoon into a greased and lined 20 cm/8 in square tin (pan) and leave to cool slightly. Cut into squares, then leave to cool completely before lifting out of the tin.

Almond Paste

Covers the top and sides of one 23 cm/9 in cake

225 g/8 oz/2 cups ground almonds

225 g/8 oz/11/3 cups icing (confectioners') sugar, sifted

225 g/8 oz/1 cup caster (superfine) sugar

2 eggs, lightly beaten

10 ml/2 tsp lemon juice

A few drops of almond essence (extract)

Beat together the almonds and sugars. Gradually blend in the remaining ingredients until you have a smooth paste. Wrap in clingfilm (plastic wrap) and chill before use.

Sugar-free Almond Paste

Covers the top and sides of one 15 cm/6 in cake

100 g/4 oz/1 cup ground almonds

50 g/2 oz/½ cup fructose

25 g/1 oz/¼ cup cornflour (cornstarch)

1 egg, lightly beaten

Blend together all the ingredients until you have a smooth paste. Wrap in clingfilm (plastic wrap) and chill before using.

Royal Icing

Covers the top and sides of one 20 cm/8 in cake

5 ml/1 tsp lemon juice

2 egg whites

450 g/1 lb/2 2/3 cups icing (confectioners') sugar, sifted

5 ml/1 tsp glycerine (optional)

Mix together the lemon juice and egg whites and gradually beat in the icing sugar until the icing (frosting) is smooth and white and will coat the back of a spoon. A few drops of glycerine will prevent the icing from becoming too brittle. Cover with a damp cloth and leave to stand for 20 minutes to allow any air bubbles to rise to the surface.

Icing of this consistency can be poured on to the cake and smoothed with a knife dipped in hot water. For piping, mix in extra icing sugar so that the icing is stiff enough to stand in peaks.

Sugar-free Icing

Makes enough to cover one 15 cm/6 in cake

50 g/2 oz/½ cup fructose

A pinch of salt

1 egg white

2.5 ml/½ tsp lemon juice

Process the fructose powder in a food processor until it is as fine as icing sugar. Blend in the salt. Transfer to a heatproof bowl and whisk in the egg white and lemon juice. Place the bowl over a pan of gently simmering water and continue to whisk until stiff peaks form. Remove from the heat and whisk until cool.

Fondant Icing

Makes enough to cover one 20 cm/8 in cake

450 g/1 lb/2 cups caster (superfine) or lump sugar

150 ml/¼ pt/2/3 cup water

15 ml/1 tbsp liquid glucose or 2.5 ml/½ tsp cream of tartar

Dissolve the sugar in the water in a large, heavy-based pan over a low heat. Wipe down the sides of the pan with a brush dipped in cold water to prevent crystals forming. Dissolve the cream of tartar in a little water, then stir into the pan. Bring to the boil and boil steadily to 115°C/242°F when a drop of icing forms a soft ball when dropped into cold water. Slowly pour the syrup into a heatproof bowl and leave until a skin forms. Beat the icing with a wooden spoon until it becomes opaque and firm. Knead until smooth. Warm in a heatproof bowl over a pan of hot water to soften, if necessary, before use.

Butter Icing

Makes enough to fill and cover one 20 cm/8 in cake

100 g/4 oz/½ cup butter or margarine, softened

225 g/ 8 oz/11/3 cups icing (confectioners') sugar, sifted

30 ml/2 tbsp milk

Beat the butter or margarine until soft. Gradually beat in the icing sugar and milk until well blended.

Chocolate Butter Icing

Makes enough to fill and cover one 20 cm/8 in cake

30 ml/2 tbsp cocoa (unsweetened chocolate) powder

15 ml/1 tbsp boiling water

100 g/4 oz/½ cup butter or margarine, softened

225 g/8 oz/11/3 cups icing (confectioners') sugar, sifted

15 ml/1 tbsp milk

Mix the cocoa to a paste with the boiling water, then leave to cool. Beat the butter or margarine until soft. Gradually beat in the icing sugar, milk and cocoa mixture until well blended.

White Chocolate Butter Icing

Makes enough to fill and cover one 20 cm/8 in cake

100 g/4 oz/1 cup white chocolate

100 g/4 oz/½ cup butter or margarine, softened

225 g/8 oz/1 1/3 cups icing (confectioners') sugar, sifted

15 ml/1 tbsp milk

Melt the chocolate in a heatproof bowl set over a pan of gently simmering water, then leave to cool slightly. Beat the butter or margarine until soft. Gradually beat in the icing sugar, milk and chocolate until well blended.

Coffee Butter Icing

Makes enough to fill and cover one 20 cm/8 in cake

100 g/4 oz/½ cup butter or margarine, softened

225 g/ 8 oz/11/3 cups icing (confectioners') sugar, sifted

15 ml/1 tbsp milk

15 ml/1 tbsp coffee essence (extract)

Beat the butter or margarine until soft. Gradually beat in the icing sugar, milk and coffee essence until well blended.

Lemon Butter Icing

Makes enough to fill and cover one 20 cm/8 in cake

100 g/4 oz/½ cup butter or margarine, softened

225 g/ 8 oz/11/3 cups icing (confectioners') sugar, sifted

30 ml/2 tbsp lemon juice

Grated rind of 1 lemon

Beat the butter or margarine until soft. Gradually beat in the icing sugar, lemon juice and rind until well blended.

Orange Butter Icing

Makes enough to fill and cover one 20 cm/8 in cake

100 g/4 oz/½ cup butter or margarine, softened

225 g/ 8 oz/1 1/3 cups icing (confectioners') sugar, sifted

30 ml/2 tbsp orange juice

Grated rind of 1 orange

Beat the butter or margarine until soft. Gradually beat in the icing sugar, orange juice and rind until well blended.

Cream Cheese Icing

Makes enough to cover one 25 cm/9 in cake

75 g/3 oz/1/3 cup cream cheese

30 ml/2 tbsp butter or margarine

350 g/12 oz/2 cups icing (confectioners') sugar, sifted

5 ml/1 tsp vanilla essence (extract)

Beat together the cheese and butter or margarine until light and fluffy. Gradually beat in the icing sugar and vanilla essence until you have a smooth, creamy icing.

Orange Icing

Makes enough to cover one 25 cm/9 in cake

250 g/9 oz/1½ cups icing (confectioners') sugar, sifted

30 ml/2 tbsp butter or margarine, softened

A few drops of almond essence (extract)

60 ml/4 tbsp orange juice

Place the icing sugar in a bowl and blend in the butter or margarine and the almond essence. Gradually blend in enough of the orange juice to make a stiff icing.

Orange Liqueur Icing

Makes enough to cover one 20 cm/8 in cake

100 g/4 oz/½ cup butter or margarine, softened

450 g/1 lb/2⅔ cups icing (confectioners') sugar, sifted

60 ml/4 tbsp orange liqueur

15 ml/1 tbsp grated orange rind

Cream together the butter or mar-garine and sugar until light and fluffy. Beat in enough of the orange liqueur to give a spreadable consistency, then stir in the orange rind.

Oat and Raisin Cookies

Makes 20

175 g/6 oz/¾ cup plain (all-purpose) flour

150 g/5 oz/1¼ cups rolled oats

5 ml/1 tsp ground ginger

2.5 ml/½ tsp baking powder

2.5 ml/½ tsp bicarbonate of soda (baking soda)

100 g/4 oz/½ cup soft brown sugar

50 g/2 oz/1/3 cup raisins

1 egg, lightly beaten

150 ml/¼ pt/2/3 cup oil

60 ml/4 tbsp milk

Mix together the dry ingredients, stir in the raisins and make a well in the centre. Add the egg, oil and milk and mix to a soft dough. Place spoonfuls of the mixture on an ungreased baking (cookie) sheet and flatten slightly with a fork. Bake in a preheated oven at 200°C/400°F/ gas mark 6 for 10 minutes until golden.

Spiced Oatmeal Biscuits

Makes 30

100 g/4 oz/½ cup butter or margarine, softened

100 g/4 oz/½ cup soft brown sugar

100 g/4 oz/½ cup caster (superfine) sugar

1 egg

2.5 ml/½ tsp vanilla essence (extract)

100 g/4 oz/1 cup plain (all-purpose) flour

2.5 ml/½ tsp bicarbonate of soda (baking soda)

A pinch of salt

5 ml/1 tsp ground cinnamon

A pinch of grated nutmeg

100 g/4 oz/1 cup rolled oats

50 g/2 oz/½ cup chopped mixed nuts

50 g/2 oz/½ cup chocolate chips

Cream together the butter or margarine and sugars until light and fluffy. Gradually beat in the egg and vanilla essence. Mix together the flour, bicarbonate of soda, salt and spices and add to the mixture. Stir in the oats, nuts and chocolate chips. Drop rounded teaspoonfuls on to a greased baking (cookie) sheet and bake the biscuits (cookies) in a preheated oven at 180°C/ 350°F/gas mark 4 for 10 minutes until lightly browned.

Wholemeal Oat Biscuits

Makes 24

100 g/4 oz/½ cup butter or margarine

200 g/7 oz/1¾ cups oatmeal

75 g/3 oz/¾ cup wholemeal (wholewheat) flour

50 g/2 oz/½ cup plain (all-purpose) flour

5 ml/1 tsp baking powder

50 g/2 oz/¼ cup demerara sugar

1 egg, lightly beaten

30 ml/2 tbsp milk

Rub the butter or margarine into the oatmeal, flours and baking powder until the mixture resembles breadcrumbs. Stir in the sugar, then mix in the egg and milk to make a stiff dough. Roll out the dough on a lightly floured surface to about 1 cm/½ in thick and cut into rounds with a 5 cm/2 in cutter. Place the biscuits (cookies) on a greased baking (cookie) sheet and bake in a preheated oven at 190°C/375°F/gas mark 5 for about 15 minutes until golden brown.

Orange Biscuits

Makes 24

100 g/4 oz/½ cup butter or margarine, softened

50 g/2 oz/¼ cup caster (superfine) sugar

Grated rind of 1 orange

150 g/5 oz/1¼ cups self-raising (self-rising) flour

Cream together the butter or margarine and sugar until light and fluffy. Work in the orange rind, then mix in the flour to make a stiff mixture. Shape into large walnut-sized balls and arrange well apart on a greased baking (cookie) sheet, then press down lightly with a fork to flatten. Bake the biscuits (cookies) in a preheated oven at 180°C/350°F/gas mark 4 for 15 minutes until golden brown.

Orange and Lemon Biscuits

Makes 30

50 g/2 oz/¼ cup butter or margarine, softened

75 g/3 oz/1/3 cup caster (superfine) sugar

1 egg yolk

Grated rind of ½ orange

15 ml/1 tbsp lemon juice

150 g/5 oz/1¼ cups plain (all-purpose) flour

2.5 ml/½ tsp baking powder

A pinch of salt

Cream together the butter or margarine and sugar until light and fluffy. Gradually mix in the egg yolk, orange rind and lemon juice, then fold in the flour, baking powder and salt to make a stiff dough. Wrap and clingfilm (plastic wrap) and chill for 30 minutes.

Roll out on a lightly floured surface to about 5 mm/¼ in thick and cut into shapes with a biscuit (cookie) cutter. Place the biscuits on a greased baking (cookie) sheet and bake in a preheated oven at 190°C/375°F/gas mark 5 for 10 minutes.

Orange and Walnut Biscuits

Makes 16

100 g/4 oz/½ cup butter or margarine

75 g/3 oz/1/3 cup caster (superfine) sugar

Grated rind of ½ orange

150 g/5 oz/1¼ cups self-raising (self-rising) flour

50 g/2 oz/½ cup walnuts, ground

Beat the butter or margarine with 50 g/2 oz/¼ cup of the sugar and the orange rind until smooth and creamy. Add the flour and nuts and beat again until the mixture begins to hold together. Form into balls and flatten on to a greased baking (cookie) sheet. Bake the biscuits (cookies) in a preheated oven at 190°C/375°F/gas mark 5 for 10 minutes until brown round the edges. Sprinkle with the reserved sugar and leave to cool slightly before transferring to a wire rack to cool.

Orange and Chocolate Chip Biscuits

Makes 30

50 g/2 oz/¼ cup butter or margarine, softened

75 g/3 oz/1/3 cup lard (shortening)

175 g/6 oz/¾ cup soft brown sugar

100 g/7 oz/1¾ cups wholemeal (wholewheat) flour

75 g/3 oz/¾ cup ground almonds

10 ml/2 tsp baking powder

75 g/3 oz/¾ cup chocolate drops

Grated rind of 2 oranges

15 ml/1 tbsp orange juice

1 egg

Caster (superfine) sugar for sprinkling

Cream together the butter or margarine, lard and brown sugar until light and fluffy. Add the remaining ingredients except the caster sugar and mix to a dough. Roll out on a floured surface to 5 mm/¼ in thick and cut into biscuits with a biscuit (cookie) cutter. Arrange on a greased baking (cookie) sheet and bake in a preheated oven at 180°C/350°F/gas mark 4 for 20 minutes until golden.

Spiced Orange Biscuits

Makes 10

225 g/8 oz/2 cups plain (all-purpose) flour

2.5 ml/½ tsp ground cinnamon

A pinch of mixed (apple pie) spice

75 g/3 oz/1/3 cup caster (superfine) sugar

150 g/5 oz/2/3 cup butter or margarine, softened

2 egg yolks

Grated rind of 1 orange

75 g/3 oz/¾ cup plain (semi-sweet) chocolate

Mix together the flour and spices, then stir in the sugar. Beat in the butter or margarine, egg yolks and orange rind and mix to a smooth dough. Wrap in clingfim (plastic wrap) and chill for 1 hour.

Spoon the dough into a piping bag fitted with a large star nozzle (tip) and pipe lengths on to a greased baking (cookie) sheet. Bake in a preheated oven at 190°C/375°F/gas mark 5 for 10 minutes until golden brown. Leave to cool.

Melt the chocolate in a heatproof bowl set over a pan of gently simmering water. Dip the ends of the biscuits into the melted chocolate and leave on a sheet of baking parchment until set.

Peanut Butter Biscuits

Makes 18

100 g/4 oz/½ cup butter or margarine, softened

100 g/4 oz/½ cup caster (superfine) sugar

100 g/4 oz/½ cup crunchy or smooth peanut butter

60 ml/4 tbsp golden (light corn) syrup

15 ml/1 tbsp milk

175 g/6 oz/1½ cups plain (all-purpose) flour

2.5 ml/½ tsp bicarbonate of soda (baking soda)

Cream together the butter or margarine and sugar until light and fluffy. Blend in the peanut butter, followed by the syrup and milk. Mix together the flour and bicarbonate of soda and blend into the mixture, then knead until smooth. Shape into a log and chill until firm.

Cut into slices 5 mm/¼ in thick and arrange on a lightly greased baking (cookie) sheet. Bake the biscuits (cookies) in a preheated oven at 180°C/350°F/gas mark 4 for 12 minutes until golden.

Peanut Butter and Chocolate Swirls

Makes 24

50 g/2 oz/¼ cup butter or margarine, softened

50 g/2 oz/¼ cup soft brown sugar

50 g/2 oz/¼ cup caster (superfine) sugar

50 g/2 oz/¼ cup smooth peanut butter

1 egg yolk

75 g/3 oz/¾ cup plain (all-purpose) flour

2.5 ml/½ tsp bicarbonate of soda (baking soda)

50 g/2 oz/½ cup plain (semi-sweet) chocolate

Cream together the butter or margarine and sugars until light and fluffy. Gradually blend in the peanut butter, then the egg yolk. Mix together the flour and bicarbonate of soda and beat into the mixture to make a firm dough. Meanwhile, melt the chocolate in a heatproof bowl set over a pan of gently simmering water. Roll out the dough to 30 x 46 cm/12 x 18 in and spread with the melted chocolate almost to the edges. Roll up from the long side, wrap in clingfilm (plastic wrap) and chill until firm.

Cut the roll into 5 mm/¼ in slices and arrange on an ungreased baking (cookie) sheet. Bake in a preheated oven at 180°C/350°F/gas mark 4 for 10 minutes until golden.

Oaty Peanut Butter Biscuits

Makes 24

75 g/3 oz/1/3 cup butter or margarine, softened

75 g/3 oz/1/3 cup peanut butter

150 g/5 oz/2/3 cup soft brown sugar

1 egg

50 g/2 oz/½ cup plain (all-purpose) flour

2.5 ml/½ tsp baking powder

A pinch of salt

A few drops of vanilla essence (extract)

75 g/3 oz/¾ cup rolled oats

40 g/1½ oz/1/3 cup chocolate chips

Cream together the butter or margarine, peanut butter and sugar until light and fluffy. Gradually beat in the egg. Fold in the flour, baking powder and salt. Stir in the vanilla essence, oats and chocolate chips. Drop spoonfuls on to a greased baking (cookie) sheet and bake the biscuits (cookies) in a preheated oven at 180°C/350°F/gas mark 4 for 15 minutes.

Honey and Coconut Peanut Butter Biscuits

Makes 24

120 ml/4 fl oz/½ cup oil

175 g/6 oz/½ cup clear honey

175 g/6 oz/¾ cup crunchy peanut butter

1 egg, beaten

100 g/4 oz/1 cup rolled oats

225 g/8 oz/2 cups wholemeal (wholewheat) flour

50 g/2 oz/½ cup desiccated (shredded) coconut

Mix together the oil, honey, peanut butter and egg, then stir in the remaining ingredients. Drop spoonfuls on to a greased baking (cookie) sheet and flatten slightly to about 6 mm/¼ in thick. Bake the biscuits (cookies) in a preheated oven at 180°C/350°F/gas mark 4 for 12 minutes until golden.

Pecan Nut Biscuits

Makes 24

100 g/4 oz/½ cup butter or margarine, softened

45 ml/3 tbsp soft brown sugar

100 g/4 oz/1 cup plain (all-purpose) flour

A pinch of salt

5 ml/1 tsp vanilla essence (extract)

100 g/4 oz/1 cup pecan nuts, finely chopped

Icing (confectioners') sugar, sifted, for dusting

Cream together the butter or margarine and sugar until light and fluffy. Gradually beat in the remaining ingredients except the icing sugar. Shape into 3 cm/1½ in balls and arrange on a greased baking (cookie) sheet. Bake the biscuits (cookies) in a preheated oven at 160°C/325°F/gas mark 3 for 15 minutes until golden. Serve dusted with icing sugar.

Pinwheel Biscuits

Makes 24

175 g/6 oz/1½ cups plain (all-purpose) flour

5 ml/1 tsp baking powder

A pinch of salt

75 g/3 oz/1/3 cup butter or margarine

75 g/3 oz/1/3 cup caster (superfine) sugar

A few drops of vanilla essence (extract)

20 ml/4 tsp water

10 ml/2 tsp cocoa (unsweetened chocolate) powder

Mix together the flour, baking powder and salt, then rub in the butter or margarine until the mixture resembles breadcrumbs. Stir in the sugar. Add the vanilla essence and water and mix to a smooth dough. Shape into a ball, then cut in half. Work the cocoa into one half of the dough. Roll out each piece of dough to a 25 x 18 cm/10 x 7 in rectangle and place one on top of the other. Roll gently so they stick together. Roll up the dough from the long side and press together gently. Wrap in clingfilm (plastic wrap) and chill for about 30 minutes.

Cut into slices 2.5 cm/1 in thick and arrange, well apart, on a greased baking (cookie) sheet. Bake the biscuits (cookies) in a preheated oven at 180°C/350°F/gas mark 4 for 15 minutes until golden.

Quick Buttermilk Biscuits

Makes 12

75 g/3 oz/1/3 cup butter or margarine

225 g/8 oz/2 cups plain (all-purpose) flour

15 ml/1 tbsp baking powder

2.5 ml/½ tsp salt

175 ml/6 fl oz/¾ cup buttermilk

Icing (confectioners') sugar, sifted, for dusting (optional)

Rub the butter or margarine into the flour, baking powder and salt until the mixture resembles breadcrumbs. Gradually add the buttermilk to make a soft dough. Roll out the mixture on a lightly floured surface to about 2 cm/¾ in thick and cut into rounds with a biscuit (cookie) cutter. Place the biscuits on a greased baking (cookie) sheet and bake in a preheated oven at 230°C/450°F/gas mark 8 for 10 minutes until golden brown. Dust with icing sugar, if liked.

Raisin Biscuits

Makes 24

100 g/4 oz/½ cup butter or margarine, softened

50 g/2 oz/¼ cup caster (superfine) sugar

Grated rind of 1 lemon

50 g/2 oz/1/3 cup raisins

150 g/5 oz/1¼ cups self-raising (self-rising) flour

Cream together the butter or margarine and sugar until light and fluffy. Work in the lemon rind, then mix in the raisins and flour to make a stiff mixture. Shape into large walnut-sized balls and arrange well apart on a greased baking (cookie) sheet, then press down lightly with a fork to flatten. Bake the biscuits (cookies) in a preheated oven at 180°C/350°F/gas mark 4 for 15 minutes until golden brown.

Soft Raisin Biscuits

Makes 36

100 g/4 oz/⅔ cup raisins

90 ml/6 tbsp boiling water

50 g/2 oz/¼ cup butter or margarine, softened

175 g/6 oz/¾ cup caster (superfine) sugar

1 egg, lightly beaten

2.5 ml/½ tsp vanilla essence (extract)

175 g/6 oz/1½ cups plain (all-purpose) flour

2.5 ml/½ tsp baking powder

1.5 ml/¼ tsp bicarbonate of soda (baking soda)

2.5 ml/½ tsp salt

2.5 ml/½ tsp ground cinnamon

A pinch of grated nutmeg

50 g/2 oz/½ cup chopped mixed nuts

Place the raisins and boiling water in a pan, bring to the boil, cover and simmer for 3 minutes. Leave to cool. Cream together the butter or margarine and sugar until light and fluffy. Gradually beat in the egg and vanilla essence. Fold in the flour, baking powder, bicarbonate of soda, salt and spices alternately with the raisins and soaking liquid. Stir in the nuts and mix to a soft dough. Wrap in clingfilm (plastic wrap) and chill for at least 1 hour.

Drop spoonfuls of dough on to a greased baking (cookie) sheet and bake the biscuits (cookies) in a preheated oven at 180°C/350°F/gas mark 4 for 10 minutes until golden.

Raisin and Treacle Slices

Makes 24

25 g/1 oz/2 tbsp butter or margarine, softened

100 g/4 oz/½ cup caster (superfine) sugar

1 egg yolk

30 ml/2 tbsp black treacle (molasses)

75 g/3 oz/½ cup currants

150 g/5 oz/1¼ cups plain (all-purpose) flour

5 ml/1 tsp bicarbonate of soda (baking soda)

5 ml/1 tsp ground cinnamon

A pinch of salt

30 ml/2 tbsp cold black coffee

Cream together the butter or margarine and sugar until light and fluffy. Gradually beat in the egg yolk and treacle, then stir in the currants. Mix together the flour, bicarbonate of soda, cinnamon and salt and stir into the mixture with the coffee. Cover and chill the mixture.

Roll out to a 30 cm/12 in square, then roll up into a log. Place on a greased baking (cookie) sheet and bake in a preheated oven at 180°C/350°F/gas mark 4 for 15 minutes until firm to the touch. Cut into slices, then leave to cool on a wire rack.

Ratafia Biscuits

Makes 16

100 g/4 oz/½ cup granulated sugar

50 g/2 oz/¼ cup ground almonds

15 ml/1 tbsp ground rice

1 egg white

25 g/1 oz/¼ cup flaked (slivered) almonds

Blend together the sugar, ground almonds and ground rice. Beat in the egg white and continue to beat for 2 minutes. Pipe walnut-sized biscuits (cookies) on to a baking (cookie) sheet lined with rice paper using a 5 mm/¼ in plain nozzle (tip). Place a flaked almond on top of each biscuit. Bake in a preheated oven at 190°C/375°F/gas mark 5 for 15 minutes until golden.

Rice and Muesli Cookies

Makes 24

75 g/3 oz/¼ cup cooked brown rice

50 g/2 oz/½ cup muesli

75 g/3 oz/¾ cup wholemeal (wholewheat) flour

2.5 ml/½ tsp salt

2.5 ml/½ tsp bicarbonate of soda (baking soda)

5 ml/1 tsp ground mixed (apple pie) spice

30 ml/2 tbsp clear honey

75 g/3 oz/1/3 cup butter or margarine, softened

Mix together the rice, muesli, flour, salt, bicarbonate of soda and mixed spice. Cream together the honey and butter or margarine until soft. Beat into the rice mixture. Shape the mixture into walnut-sized balls and place well apart on greased baking (cookie) sheets. Flatten slightly, then bake in a preheated oven at 190°C/375°F/gas mark 5 for 15 minutes or until golden brown. Leave to cool for 10 minutes, then transfer to a wire rack to finish cooling. Store in an airtight container.

Romany Creams

Makes 10

25 g/1 oz/2 tbsp lard (shortening)

25 g/1 oz/2 tbsp butter or margarine, softened

50 g/2 oz/¼ cup soft brown sugar

2.5 ml/½ tsp golden (light corn) syrup

50 g/2 oz/½ cup plain (all-purpose) flour

A pinch of salt

25 g/1 oz/¼ cup rolled oats

2.5 ml/½ tsp ground mixed (apple-pie) spice

2.5 ml/½ tsp bicarbonate of soda (baking soda)

10 ml/2 tsp boiling water

Butter Icing

Cream together the lard, butter or margarine and sugar until light and fluffy. Beat in the syrup, then add the flour, salt, oats and mixed spice and stir until well blended. Dissolve the bicarbonate of soda in the water and mix in to make a firm dough. Shape into 20 equal-sized small balls and place well apart on greased baking (cookie) sheets. Flatten slightly with the palm of your hand. Bake in a preheated oven at 160°C/325°F/gas mark 3 for 15 minutes. Leave to cool on the baking sheets. When cool, sandwich pairs of biscuits together with the butter icing (frosting).

Sand Biscuits

Makes 48

100 g/4 oz/½ cup butter or hard margarine, softened

225 g/8 oz/1 cup soft brown sugar

1 egg, lightly beaten

225 g/8 oz/2 cups plain (all-purpose) flour

Egg white to glaze

30 ml/2 tbsp crushed peanuts

Cream together the butter or margarine and sugar until light and fluffy. Beat in the egg, then blend in the flour. Roll out very thinly on a lightly floured surface and cut into shapes with a biscuit (cookie) cutter. Place the biscuits on a greased baking (cookie) sheet, brush the tops with egg white and sprinkle with peanuts. Bake in a preheated oven at 180°C/350°F/gas mark 4 for 10 minutes until golden.

Soured Cream Cookies

Makes 24

50 g/2 oz/¼ cup butter or margarine, softened

175 g/6 oz/¾ cup caster (superfine) sugar

1 egg

60 ml/4 tbsp soured (dairy sour) cream

2. 5 ml/½ tsp vanilla essence (extract)

150 g/5 oz/1¼ cups plain (all-purpose) flour

2.5 ml/½ tsp baking powder

75 g/3 oz/½ cup raisins

Cream together the butter or margarine and sugar until light and fluffy. Gradually beat in the egg, cream and vanilla essence. Mix together the flour, baking powder and raisins and stir into the mixture until well blended. Drop rounded teaspoonfuls of the mixture on to lightly greased baking (cookie) sheets and bake in a preheated oven at 180°C/ 350°F/gas mark 4 for about 10 minutes until just golden.

Brown Sugar Biscuits

Makes 24

100 g/4 oz/½ cup butter or margarine, softened

100 g/4 oz/½ cup soft brown sugar

1 egg, lightly beaten

2.5 ml/1 tsp vanilla essence (extract)

150 g/5 oz/1¼ cups plain (all-purpose) flour

2.5 ml/½ tsp bicarbonate of soda (baking soda)

A pinch of salt

75 g/3 oz/½ cup sultanas (golden raisins)

Cream together the butter or margarine and sugar until light and fluffy. Gradually beat in the egg and vanilla essence. Stir in the remaining ingredients until smooth. Drop rounded teaspoonfuls well apart on to a lightly greased baking (cookie) sheet. Bake the biscuits (cookies) in a preheated oven at 180°C/ 350°F/gas mark 4 for 12 minutes until golden brown.

Sugar and Nutmeg Biscuits

Makes 24

50 g/2 oz/¼ cup butter or margarine, softened

100 g/4 oz/½ cup caster (superfine) sugar

1 egg yolk

2.5 ml/½ tsp vanilla essence (extract)

150 g/5 oz/1¼ cups plain (all-purpose) flour

5 ml/1 tsp baking powder

A pinch of grated nutmeg

60 ml/4 tbsp soured (dairy sour) cream

Cream together the butter or margarine and sugar until light and fluffy. Beat in the egg yolk and vanilla essence, then stir in the flour, baking powder and nutmeg. Blend in the cream until smooth. Cover and chill for 30 minutes.

Roll out the dough to 5 mm/¼ in thick and cut into 5 cm/2 in rounds with a biscuit (cookie) cutter. Place the biscuits on an ungreased baking (cookie) sheet and bake in a preheated oven at 200°C/ 400°F/gas mark 6 for 10 minutes until golden.

Shortbread

Makes 8

150 g/5 oz/1¼ cups plain (all-purpose) flour

A pinch of salt

25 g/1 oz/¼ cup rice flour or ground rice

50 g/2 oz/¼ cup caster (superfine) sugar

100 g/4 oz/¼ cup butter or hard margarine, chilled and grated

Mix together the flour, salt and rice flour or ground rice. Stir in the sugar, then the butter or margarine. Work the mixture with the fingertips until it resembles breadcrumbs. Press into an 18 cm/7 in sandwich tin (pan) and level the top. Prick all over with a fork and mark into eight equal wedges, cutting through to the base. Chill for 1 hour.

Bake in a preheated oven at 150°C/ 300°F/gas mark 2 for 1 hour until pale straw-coloured. Leave to cool in the tin before turning out.

Christmas Shortbread

Makes 12

175 g/6 oz/¾ cup butter or margarine

250 g/9 oz/2¼ cups plain (all-purpose) flour

75 g/3 oz/1/3 cup caster (superfine) sugar

For the topping:

15 ml/1 tbsp almonds, chopped

15 ml/1 tbsp walnuts, chopped

30 ml/2 tbsp raisins

30 ml/2 tbsp glacé (candied) cherries, chopped

Grated rind of 1 lemon

15 ml/1 tbsp caster (superfine) sugar for sprinkling

Rub the butter or margarine into the flour until the mixture resembles breadcrumbs. Stir in the sugar. Press the mixture together to a paste and knead until smooth. Press into a greased Swiss roll tin (jelly roll pan) and level the surface. Mix together the topping ingredients and press them into the paste. Mark into 12 fingers, then bake in a preheated oven at 180°C/350°F/gas mark 4 for 30 minutes. Sprinkle with caster sugar, cut into fingers and leave to cool in the tin.

Honeyed Shortbread

Makes 12

100 g/4 oz/½ cup butter or margarine, softened

75 g/3 oz/¼ cup set honey

200 g/7 oz/1¾ cups wholemeal (wholewheat) flour

25 g/1 oz/¼ cup brown rice flour

Grated rind of 1 lemon

Cream together the butter or margarine and honey until soft. Stir in the flours and lemon rind and work to a soft dough. Press into a greased and floured 18 cm/7 in cake tin (pan) or shortbread mould and prick all over with a fork. Mark into 12 wedges and crimp the edges. Chill for 1 hour.

Bake in a preheated oven at 150°C/ 300°F/gas mark 2 for 40 minutes until just golden. Cut into the marked pieces and leave to cool in the tin.

Lemon Shortbread

Makes 12

100 g/4 oz/1 cup plain (all-purpose) flour

50 g/2 oz/½ cup cornflour (cornstarch)

100 g/4 oz/½ cup butter or margarine, softened

50 g/2 oz/¼ cup caster (superfine) sugar

Grated rind of 1 lemon

Caster (superfine) sugar for sprinkling

Sift the flour and cornflour together. Cream the butter or margarine until soft, then beat in the caster sugar until pale and fluffy. Stir in the lemon rind, then beat in the flour mixture until well blended. Roll out the shortbread to a 20 cm/8 in circle and place on a greased baking (cookie) sheet. Prick all over with a fork and flute the edges. Cut into 12 wedges, then sprinkle with caster sugar. Chill in the fridge for 15 minutes. Bake in a preheated oven at 160°C/325°F/gas mark 3 for 35 minutes until pale golden brown. Leave to cool on the baking sheet for 5 minutes before turning out on to a wire rack to finish cooling.

Mincemeat Shortbread

Makes 8

175 g/6 oz/¾ cup butter or margarine, softened

50 g/2 oz/¼ cup caster (superfine) sugar

225 g/8 oz/2 cups plain (all-purpose) flour

60 ml/4 tbsp mincemeat

Cream the butter or margarine and sugar until soft. Work in the flour, then the mincemeat. Press into a 23 cm/ 7 in sandwich tin and level the top. Prick all over with a fork and mark into eight wedges, cutting through to the base. Chill for 1 hour.

Bake in a preheated oven at 160°C/ 325°F/gas mark 3 for 1 hour until pale straw-coloured. Leave to cool in the tin before turning out.

Nut Shortbread

Makes 12

100 g/4 oz/½ cup butter or margarine, softened

50 g/2 oz/¼ cup caster (superfine) sugar

100 g/4 oz/1 cup plain (all-purpose) flour

50 g/2 oz/½ cup ground rice

50 g/2 oz/½ cup almonds, finely chopped

Beat together the butter or margarine and sugar until light and fluffy. Mix in the flour and ground rice. Stir in the nuts and mix to a firm dough. Knead lightly until smooth. Press into the base of a greased Swiss roll tin (jelly roll pan) and level the surface. Prick all over with a fork. Bake in a preheated oven at 160°C/325°F/ gas mark 3 for 45 minutes until pale golden brown. Leave to cool in the tin for 10 minutes, then cut into fingers. Leave in the tin to finish cooling before turning out.

Orange Shortbread

Makes 12

100 g/4 oz/1 cup plain (all-purpose) flour

50 g/2 oz/½ cup cornflour (cornstarch)

100 g/4 oz/½ cup butter or margarine, softened

50 g/2 oz/¼ cup caster (superfine) sugar

Grated rind of 1 orange

Caster (superfine) sugar for sprinkling

Sift the flour and cornflour together. Cream the butter or margarine until soft, then beat in the caster sugar until pale and fluffy. Stir in the orange rind, then beat in the flour mixture until well blended. Roll out the shortbread to a 20 cm/8 in circle and place on a greased baking (cookie) sheet. Prick all over with a fork and flute the edges. Cut into 12 wedges, then sprinkle with caster sugar. Chill in the fridge for 15 minutes. Bake in a preheated oven at 160°C/325°F/gas mark 3 for 35 minutes until pale golden brown. Leave to cool on the baking sheet for 5 minutes before turning out on to a wire rack to finish cooling.

Rich Man's Shortbread

Makes 36

For the base:

225 g/8 oz/1 cup butter or margarine

275 g/10 oz/2½ cups plain (all-purpose) flour

100 g/4 oz/½ cup caster (superfine) sugar

For the filling:

225 g/8 oz/1 cup butter or margarine

225 g/8 oz/1 cup soft brown sugar

60 ml/4 tbsp golden (light corn) syrup

400 g/14 oz canned condensed milk

A few drops of vanilla essence (extract)

For the topping:

225 g/8 oz/2 cups plain (semi-sweet) chocolate

To make the base, rub the butter or margarine into the flour, then stir in the sugar and knead the mixture to a firm dough. Press into the base of a greased Swiss roll tin (jelly roll pan) lined with foil. Bake in a preheated oven at 180°C/ 350°F/gas mark 4 for 35 minutes until golden. Leave in the tin to cool.

To make the filling, melt the butter or margarine, sugar, syrup and condensed milk in a pan over a low heat, stirring continuously. Bring to the boil, then simmer gently, stirring continuously, for 7 minutes. Remove from the heat, add the vanilla essence and beat thoroughly. Pour over the base and leave to cool and set.

Melt the chocolate in a heatproof bowl set over a pan of gently simmering water. Spread over the caramel layer and mark into patterns with a fork. Leave to cool and set, then cut into squares.

Wholemeal Oat Shortbread

Makes 10

100 g/4 oz/½ cup butter or margarine

150 g/5 oz/1¼ cups wholemeal (wholewheat) flour

25 g/1 oz/¼ cup oat flour

50 g/2 oz/¼ cup soft brown sugar

Rub the butter or margarine into the flours until the mixture resembles breadcrumbs. Stir in the sugar and lightly work to a soft, crumbly dough. Roll out on a lightly floured surface to about 1 cm/½ in thick and cut into 5 cm/2 in rounds with a biscuit (cookie) cutter. Transfer carefully to a greased baking (cookie) sheet and bake in a preheated oven at 150°C/300°F/gas mark 3 for about 40 minutes until golden and firm.

Almond Whirls

Makes 16

175 g/6 oz/¾ cup butter or margarine, softened

50 g/2 oz/1/3 cup icing (confectioners') sugar, sifted

2.5 ml/½ tsp almond essence (extract)

175 g/6 oz/1½ cups plain (all-purpose) flour

8 glacé (candied) cherries, halved or quartered

Icing (confectioners') sugar, sifted, for dusting

Cream together the butter or margarine and sugar. Beat in the almond essence and flour. Transfer the mixture to a piping bag fitted with a large star-shaped nozzle (tip). Pipe 16 flat whirls on to a greased baking (cookie) sheet. Top each one with a piece of cherry. Bake in a preheated oven at 160°C/325°F/gas mark 3 for 20 minutes until pale golden. Leave on the tray to cool for 5 minutes then transfer to a wire rack and dust with icing sugar.

Chocolate Meringue Shortbread

Makes 24

100 g/4 oz/½ cup butter or margarine, softened

5 ml/1 tsp vanilla essence (extract)

4 egg whites

200 g/7 oz/1¾ cups plain (all-purpose) flour

50 g/2 oz/¼ cup caster (superfine) sugar

45 ml/3 tbsp cocoa (unsweetened chocolate) powder

100 g/4 oz/2/3 cup icing (confectioners') sugar, sifted

Beat together the butter or margarine, vanilla essence and two of the egg whites. Mix together the flour, sugar and cocoa, then gradually beat into the butter mixture. Press into a greased 30 cm/12 in square tin (pan). Beat together the remaining egg whites with the icing sugar and spread over the top. Bake in a preheated oven at 190°C/375°F/gas mark 5 for 20 minutes until golden brown. Cut into bars.

Biscuit People

Makes about 12

100 g/4 oz/½ cup butter or margarine, softened

100 g/4 oz/½ cup caster (superfine) sugar

1 egg, beaten

225 g/8 oz/2 cups plain (all-purpose) flour

A few currants and glacé (candied) cherries

Cream together the butter or margarine and sugar. Gradually add the egg and beat thoroughly. Fold in the flour using a metal spoon. Roll out the mixture on a lightly floured surface to about 5 mm/¼ in thick. Cut out people with a biscuit (cookie) cutter or knife, re-rolling the trimmings until you have used all the dough. Place on a greased baking (cookie) sheet and press in currants for eyes and buttons. Cut slices of cherry for the mouths. Bake the biscuits (cookies) in a preheated oven at 190°C/375°F/gas mark 5 for 10 minutes until pale brown. Leave to cool on a wire rack.

Iced Ginger Shortcake

Makes two 20 cm/8 in cakes

For the shortcake:

225 g/8 oz/1 cup butter or margarine, softened

100 g/4 oz/½ cup caster (superfine) sugar

275 g/10 oz/2½ cups plain (all-purpose) flour

10 ml/2 tsp baking powder

10 ml/2 tsp ground ginger

For the icing (frosting):

50 g/2 oz/¼ cup butter or margarine

15 ml/1 tbsp golden (light corn) syrup

100 g/4 oz/2/3 cup icing (confectioners') sugar, sifted

5 ml/1 tsp ground ginger

To make the shortcake, cream together the butter or margarine and sugar until light and fluffy. Mix in the remaining shortcake ingredients to make a dough, divide the mixture in half and press into two greased 20 cm/8 in sandwich tins (pans). Bake in a preheated oven at 160°C/325°F/gas mark 3 for 40 minutes.

To make the icing, melt the butter or margarine and syrup in a pan. Add the icing sugar and ginger and blend together well. Pour over both shortcakes and leave until cool, then cut into wedges.

Shrewsbury Biscuits

Makes 24

100 g/4 oz/½ cup butter or margarine, softened

100 g/4 oz/½ cup caster (superfine) sugar

1 egg yolk

225 g/8 oz/2 cups plain (all-purpose) flour

5 ml/1 tsp baking powder

5 ml/1 tsp grated lemon rind

Cream together the butter or margarine and sugar until light and fluffy. Gradually beat in the egg yolk, then work in the flour, baking powder and lemon rind, finishing with your hands until the mixture binds together. Roll out to 5 mm/ ¼ in thick and cut into 6 cm/2¼ in rounds with a biscuit (cookie) cutter. Place the biscuits well apart on a greased baking (cookie) sheet and prick them with a fork. Bake in a preheated oven at 180°C/350°F/ gas mark 4 for 15 minutes until pale golden.

Spanish Spiced Biscuits

Makes 16

90 ml/6 tbsp olive oil

100 g/4 oz/½ cup granulated sugar

100 g/4 oz/1 cup plain (all-purpose) flour

15 ml/1 tbsp baking powder

10 ml/2 tsp ground cinnamon

3 eggs

Grated rind of 1 lemon

30 ml/2 tbsp icing (confectioners') sugar, sifted

Warm the oil in a small pan. Mix together the sugar, flour, baking powder and cinnamon. In a separate bowl, beat the eggs and lemon rind until frothy. Stir in the dry ingredients and oil to make a smooth batter. Pour the batter into a well-greased Swiss roll tin (jelly roll pan) and bake in a preheated oven at 180°C/350°F/gas mark 4 for 30 minutes until golden. Turn out, leave to cool, then cut into triangles and sprinkle the biscuits (cookies) with icing sugar.

Old-fashioned Spice Biscuits

Makes 24

75 g/3 oz/1/3 cup butter or margarine

50 g/2 oz/¼ cup caster (superfine) sugar

45 ml/3 tbsp black treacle (molasses)

175 g/6 oz/¾ cup plain (all-purpose) flour

5 ml/1 tsp ground cinnamon

5 ml/1 tsp ground mixed (apple-pie) spice

2.5 ml/½ tsp ground ginger

2.5 ml/½ tsp bicarbonate of soda (baking soda)

Melt the butter or margarine, sugar and treacle together over a low heat. Mix together the flour, spices and bicarbonate of soda in a bowl. Pour into the treacle mixture and mix together until well blended. Blend to a soft dough and shape into small balls. Arrange, well apart, on a greased baking (cookie) sheet and press flat with a fork. Bake the biscuits (cookies) in a preheated oven at 180°C/350°F/gas mark 4 for 12 minutes until firm and golden.

Treacle Biscuits

Makes 24

75 g/3 oz/1/3 cup butter or margarine, softened

100 g/4 oz/½ cup soft brown sugar

1 egg yolk

30 ml/2 tbsp black treacle (molasses)

100 g/4 oz/1 cup plain (all-purpose) flour

5 ml/1 tsp bicarbonate of soda (baking soda)

A pinch of salt

5 ml/1 tsp ground cinnamon

2.5 ml/½ tsp ground cloves

Beat together the butter or margarine and sugar until light and fluffy. Gradually beat in the egg yolk and molasses. Mix together the flour, bicarbonate of soda, salt and spices and blend into the mixture. Cover and chill.

Roll the mixture into 3 cm/1½ in balls and arrange on a greased baking (cookie) sheet. Bake the biscuits (cookies) in a preheated oven at 180°C/350°F/gas mark 4 for 10 minutes until just set.

Treacle, Apricot and Nut Cookies

Makes about 24

50 g/2 oz/¼ cup butter or margarine

50 g/2 oz/¼ cup caster (superfine) sugar

50 g/2 oz/¼ cup soft brown sugar

1 egg, lightly beaten

2.5 ml/½ tsp bicarbonate of soda (baking soda)

30 ml/2 tbsp warm water

45 ml/3 tbsp black treacle (molasses)

25 g/1 oz ready-to-eat dried apricots, chopped

25 g/1 oz/¼ cup chopped mixed nuts

100 g/4 oz/1 cup plain (all-purpose) flour

A pinch of salt

A pinch of ground cloves

Cream together the butter or margarine and sugars until light and fluffy. Gradually beat in the egg. Mix the bicarbonate of soda with the water, the stir into the mixture with the remaining ingredients. Drop spoonfuls on to a greased baking (cookie) sheet and bake in a preheated oven at 180°C/350°F/gas mark 4 for 10 minutes.

Treacle and Buttermilk Cookies

Makes 24

50 g/2 oz/¼ cup butter or margarine, softened

50 g/2 oz/¼ cup soft brown sugar

150 ml/¼ pt/2/3 cup black treacle (molasses)

150 ml/¼ pt/2/3 cup buttermilk

175 g/6 oz/1½ cups plain (all-purpose) flour

2.5 ml/½ tsp bicarbonate of soda (baking soda)

Cream together the butter or margarine and sugar until light and fluffy, then mix in the treacle and buttermilk alternately with the flour and bicarbonate of soda. Drop large spoonfuls on to a greased baking (cookie) sheet and bake in a preheated oven at 190°C/375°F/ gas mark 5 for 10 minutes.

Treacle and Coffee Biscuits

Makes 24

60 g/2½ oz/1/3 cup lard (shortening)

50 g/2 oz/¼ cup soft brown sugar

75 g/3 oz/¼ cup black treacle (molasses)

2.5 ml/½ tsp vanilla essence (extract)

200 g/7 oz/1¾ cups plain (all-purpose) flour

5 ml/1 tsp bicarbonate of soda (baking soda)

A pinch of salt

2.5 ml/½ tsp ground ginger

2.5 ml/½ tsp ground cinnamon

60 ml/4 tbsp cold black coffee

Cream together the lard and sugar until light and fluffy. Stir in the treacle and vanilla essence. Mix together the flour, bicarbonate of soda, salt and spices and beat into the mixture alternately with the coffee. Cover and chill for several hours.

Roll out the dough to 5 mm/¼ in thick and cut into 5 cm/2 in rounds with a biscuit (cookie) cutter. Place the biscuits on an ungreased baking (cookie) sheet and bake in a preheated oven at 190°C/375°F/gas mark 5 for 10 minutes until firm to the touch.

Treacle and Date Cookies

Makes about 24

50 g/2 oz/¼ cup butter or margarine, softened

50 g/2 oz/¼ cup caster (superfine) sugar

50 g/2 oz/¼ cup soft brown sugar

1 egg, lightly beaten

2.5 ml/½ tsp bicarbonate of soda (baking soda)

30 ml/2 tbsp warm water

45 ml/3 tbsp black treacle (molasses)

25 g/1 oz/¼ cup stoned (pitted) dates, chopped

100 g/4 oz/1 cup plain (all-purpose) flour

A pinch of salt

A pinch of ground cloves

Cream together the butter or margarine and sugars until light and fluffy. Gradually beat in the egg. Mix the bicarbonate of soda with the water, then stir into the mixture with the remaining ingredients. Drop spoonfuls on to a greased baking (cookie) sheet and bake in a preheated oven at 180°C/350°F/gas mark 4 for 10 minutes.

Treacle and Ginger Cookies

Makes 24

50 g/2 oz/¼ cup butter or margarine, softened

50 g/2 oz/¼ cup soft brown sugar

150 ml/¼ pt/2/3 cup black treacle (molasses)

150 ml/¼ pt/2/3 cup buttermilk

175 g/6 oz/1½ cups plain (all-purpose) flour

2.5 ml/½ tsp bicarbonate of soda (baking soda)

2.5 ml/½ tsp ground ginger

1 egg, beaten, to glaze

Cream together the butter or margarine and sugar until light and fluffy, then mix in the treacle and buttermilk alternately with the flour, bicarbonate of soda and ground ginger. Drop large spoonfuls on to a greased baking (cookie) sheet and brush the tops with beaten egg. Bake in a preheated oven at 190°C/375°F/ gas mark 5 for 10 minutes.

Vanilla Biscuits

Makes 24

150 g/5 oz/2/3 cup butter or margarine, softened

100 g/4 oz/½ cup caster (superfine) sugar

1 egg, beaten

225 g/8 oz/2 cups self-raising (self-rising) flour

A pinch of salt

10 ml/2 tsp vanilla essence (extract)

Glacé (candied) cherries to decorate

Cream together the butter or margarine and sugar until light and fluffy. Gradually beat in the egg, then fold in the flour, salt and vanilla essence and mix to a dough. Knead until smooth. Wrap in clingfim (plastic wrap) and chill for 20 minutes.

Roll out the dough thinly and cut into rounds with a biscuit (cookie) cutter. Arrange on a greased baking (cookie) sheet and place a cherry on top of each one. Bake the biscuits in a preheated oven at 180°C/350°F/gas mark 4 for 10 minutes until golden brown. Leave to cool on the baking sheet for 10 minutes before transferring to a wire rack to finish cooling.

Walnut Biscuits

Makes 36

100 g/4 oz/½ cup butter or margarine, softened

100 g/4 oz/½ cup soft brown sugar

100 g/4 oz/½ cup caster (superfine) sugar

1 large egg, lightly beaten

200 g/7 oz/1¾ cups plain (all-purpose) flour

5 ml/1 tsp baking powder

2.5 ml/½ tsp bicarbonate of soda (baking soda)

120 ml/4 fl oz/½ cup buttermilk

50 g/2 oz/½ cup walnuts, chopped

Cream together the butter or margarine and sugars. Gradually beat in the egg, then fold in the flour, baking powder and bicarbonate of soda alternately with the buttermilk. Fold in the walnuts. Drop small spoonfuls on to a greased baking (cookie) sheet and bake the biscuits (cookies) in a preheated oven at 190°C/375°F/gas mark 5 for 10 minutes.

Crisp Biscuits

Makes 24

25 g/1 oz fresh yeast or 40 ml/ 2½ tbsp dried yeast

450 ml/¾ pt/2 cups warm milk

900 g/2 lb/8 cups strong plain (bread) flour

175 g/6 oz/¾ cup butter or margarine, softened

30 ml/2 tbsp clear honey

2 eggs, beaten

Beaten egg for glazing

Mix the yeast with a little of the warm milk and leave in a warm place for 20 minutes. Place the flour in a bowl and rub in the butter or margarine. Blend in the yeast mixture, the remaining warm milk, the honey and eggs and mix to a soft dough. Knead on a lightly floured surface until smooth and elastic. Place in an oiled bowl, cover with oiled clingfilm (plastic wrap) and leave in a warm place for 1 hour until doubled in size.

Knead again, then shape into long flat rolls and place on a greased baking (cookie) sheet. Cover with oiled clingfilm and leave in a warm place for 20 minutes.

Brush with beaten egg and bake in a preheated oven at 200°C/400°F/gas mark 6 for 20 minutes. Leave to cool overnight.

Slice thinly, then bake again in a preheated oven at 150°C/300°F/gas mark 2 for 30 minutes until crisp and brown.

Cheddar Biscuits

Makes 12

50 g/2 oz/¼ cup butter or margarine

200 g/7 oz/1¾ cups plain (all-purpose) flour

15 ml/1 tbsp baking powder

A pinch of salt

50 g/2 oz/½ cup Cheddar cheese, grated

175 ml/6 fl oz/¾ cup milk

Rub the butter or margarine into the flour, baking powder and salt until the mixture resembles breadcrumbs. Stir in the cheese, then mix in enough of the milk to make a soft dough. Roll out on a lightly floured surface to about 2 cm/ ¾ in thick and cut into rounds with a biscuit (cookie) cutter. Arrange on an ungreased baking (cookie) sheet and bake the biscuits (crackers) in a preheated oven at 200°C/400°F/gas mark 6 for 15 minutes until golden brown.

Blue Cheese Biscuits

Makes 12

50 g/2 oz/¼ cup butter or margarine

200 g/7 oz/1¾ cups plain (all-purpose) flour

15 ml/1 tbsp baking powder

50 g/2 oz/½ cup Stilton cheese, grated or crumbled

175 ml/6 fl oz/¾ cup milk

Rub the butter or margarine into the flour and baking powder until the mixture resembles breadcrumbs. Stir in the cheese, then mix in enough of the milk to make a soft dough. Roll out on a lightly floured surface to about 2 cm/ ¾ in thick and cut into rounds with a biscuit (cookie) cutter. Arrange on an ungreased baking (cookie) sheet and bake the biscuits (crackers) in a preheated oven at 200°C/400°F/gas mark 6 for 15 minutes until golden brown.

Cheese and Sesame Biscuits

Makes 24

75 g/3 oz/1/3 cup butter or margarine

75 g/3 oz/¾ cup wholemeal (wholewheat) flour

75 g/3 oz/¾ cup Cheddar cheese, grated

30 ml/2 tbsp sesame seeds

Salt and freshly ground black pepper

1 egg, beaten

Rub the butter or margarine into the flour until the mixture resembles breadcrumbs. Stir in the cheese and half the sesame seeds and season with salt and pepper. Press together to form a firm dough. Roll out the dough on a lightly floured surface to about 5 mm/¼ in thick and cut into rounds with a biscuit (cookie) cutter. Place the biscuits (crackers) on a greased baking (cookie) sheet, brush with egg and sprinkle with the remaining sesame seeds. Bake in a preheated oven at 190°C/375°F/gas mark 5 for 10 minutes until golden.

Cheese Straws

Makes 16

225 g/8 oz Puff Pastry

1 egg, beaten

100 g/4 oz/1 cup Cheddar or strong cheese, grated

15 ml/1 tbsp grated Parmesan cheese

Salt and freshly ground black pepper

Roll out the pastry (paste) to about 5 mm/¼ in thick and brush generously with beaten egg. Sprinkle with the cheeses and season to taste with salt and pepper. Cut into strips and twist the strips gently into spirals. Place on a dampened baking (cookie) sheet and bake in a preheated oven at 220°C/425°F/gas mark 7 for about 10 minutes until puffed and golden.

Cheese and Tomato Biscuits

Makes 12

50 g/2 oz/¼ cup butter or margarine

200 g/7 oz/1¾ cups plain (all-purpose) flour

15 ml/1 tbsp baking powder

A pinch of salt

50 g/2 oz/½ cup Cheddar cheese, grated

15 ml/1 tbsp tomato purée (paste)

150 ml/¼ pt/2/3 cup milk

Rub the butter or margarine into the flour, baking powder and salt until the mixture resembles breadcrumbs. Stir in the cheese, then mix in the tomato purée and enough of the milk to make a soft dough. Roll out on a lightly floured surface to about 2 cm/¾ in thick and cut into rounds with a biscuit (cookie) cutter. Arrange on an ungreased baking (cookie) sheet and bake the biscuits (crackers) in a preheated oven at 200°C/400°F/gas mark 6 for 15 minutes until golden brown.

Goats' Cheese Bites

Makes 30

2 sheets frozen filo pastry (paste), thawed

50 g/2 oz/¼ cup unsalted butter, melted

50 g/2 oz/½ cup goats' cheese, diced

5 ml/1 tsp Herbes de Provence

Brush a filo pastry sheet with melted butter, place the second sheet on top and brush with butter. Cut into 30 equal squares, place a piece of cheese on each one and sprinkle with herbs. Bring the corners together and twist to seal, then brush again with melted butter. Place on a greased baking (cookie) sheet and bake in a preheated oven at 180°C/350°F/gas mark 4 for 10 minutes until crisp and golden.

Ham and Mustard Rolls

Makes 16

225 g/8 oz Puff Pastry

30 ml/2 tbsp French mustard

100 g/4 oz/1 cup cooked ham, chopped

Salt and freshly ground black pepper

Roll out the pastry (paste) to about 5 mm/¼ in thick. Spread with the mustard, then sprinkle with the ham and season with salt and pepper. Roll up the pastry into a long sausage shape, then cut into 1 cm/½ in slices and arrange on a dampened baking (cookie) sheet. Bake in a preheated oven at 220°C/425°F/gas mark 7 for about 10 minutes until puffed and golden.

Ham and Pepper Biscuits

Makes 30

225 g/8 oz/2 cups plain (all-purpose) flour

15 ml/1 tbsp baking powder

5 ml/1 tsp dried thyme

5 ml/1 tsp caster (superfine) sugar

2.5 ml/½ tsp ground ginger

A pinch of grated nutmeg

A pinch of bicarbonate of soda (baking soda)

Salt and freshly ground black pepper

50 g/2 oz/¼ cup vegetable fat (shortening)

50 g/2 oz/½ cup cooked ham, minced

30 ml/2 tbsp finely chopped green (bell) pepper

175 ml/6 fl oz/¾ cup buttermilk

Mix together the flour, baking powder, thyme, sugar, ginger, nutmeg, bicarbonate of soda, salt and pepper. Rub in the vegetable fat until the mixture resembles breadcrumbs. Stir in the ham and pepper. Gradually add the buttermilk and mix to a soft dough. Knead for a few seconds on a lightly floured surface until smooth. Roll out to 2 cm/¾ in thick and cut into rounds with a biscuit (cookie) cutter. Place the biscuits, well apart, on a greased baking (cookie) sheet and bake in a preheated oven at 220°C/425°F/gas mark 7 for 12 minutes until puffed and golden.

Simple Herb Biscuits

Makes 8

225 g/8 oz/2 cups plain (all-purpose) flour

15 ml/1 tbsp baking powder

5 ml/1 tsp caster (superfine) sugar

2.5 ml/½ tsp salt

50 g/2 oz/¼ cup butter or margarine

15 ml/1 tbsp snipped fresh chives

A pinch of paprika

Freshly ground black pepper

45 ml/3 tbsp milk

45 ml/3 tbsp water

Mix together the flour, baking powder, sugar and salt. Rub in the butter or margarine until the mixture resembles breadcrumbs. Mix in the chives, paprika and pepper to taste. Stir in the milk and water and mix to a soft dough. Knead on a lightly floured surface until smooth, then roll out to 2 cm/¾ in thick and cut into rounds with a biscuit (cookie) cutter. Place the biscuits (crackers), well apart, on a greased baking (cookie) sheet and bake in a preheated oven at 200°C/400°F/gas mark 6 for 15 minutes until puffed and golden.

Indian Biscuits

Serves 4

100 g/4 oz/1 cup plain (all-purpose) flour

100 g/4 oz/1 cup semolina (cream of wheat)

175 g/6 oz/¾ cup caster (superfine) sugar

75 g/3 oz/¾ cup gram flour

175 g/6 oz/¾ cup ghee

Mix together all the ingredients in a bowl, then rub them with the palms of your hands to form a stiff dough. You may need a little more ghee if the mixture is too dry. Shape into small balls and press into biscuit (cracker) shapes. Place on a greased and lined baking (cookie) sheet and bake in a preheated oven at 150°C/300°F/gas mark 2 for 30–40 minutes until lightly browned. Fine hairline cracks may appear as the biscuits are cooked.

Hazelnut and Shallot Shortbread

Makes 12

75 g/3 oz/1/3 cup butter or margarine, softened

175 g/6 oz/1½ cups wholemeal (wholewheat) flour

10 ml/2 tsp baking powder

1 shallot, finely chopped

50 g/2 oz/½ cup hazelnuts, chopped

10 ml/2 tsp paprika

15 ml/1 tbsp cold water

Rub the butter or margarine into the flour and baking powder until the mixture resembles breadcrumbs. Stir in the shallot, hazelnuts and paprika. Add the cold water and press together to make a dough. Roll out and press into a 30 x 20 cm/12 x 8 in Swiss roll tin (jelly roll pan) and prick all over with a fork. Mark into fingers. Bake in a preheated oven at 200°C/400°F/gas mark 6 for 10 minutes until golden.

Salmon and Dill Biscuits

Makes 12

225 g/8 oz/2 cups plain (all-purpose) flour

5 ml/1 tsp caster (superfine) sugar

2.5 ml/½ tsp salt

20 ml/4 tsp baking powder

100 g/4 oz/½ cup butter or margarine, diced

90 ml/6 tbsp water

90 ml/6 tbsp milk

100 g/4 oz/1 cup smoked salmon trimmings, diced

60 ml/4 tbsp chopped fresh dill (dill weed)

Mix together the flour, sugar, salt and baking powder, then rub in the butter or margarine until the mixture resembles breadcrumbs. Gradually mix in the milk and water and mix to a soft dough. Work in the salmon and dill and mix until smooth. Roll out to 2.5 cm/1 in thick and cut into rounds with a biscuit (cookie) cutter. Place the biscuits (crackers) well apart on a greased baking (cookie) sheet and bake in a preheated oven at 220°C/425°F/gas mark 7 for 15 minutes until puffed and golden.

Soda Biscuits

Makes 12

45 ml/3 tbsp lard (shortening)

225 g/8 oz/2 cups plain (all-purpose) flour

5 ml/1 tsp bicarbonate of soda (baking soda)

5 ml/1 tsp cream of tartar

A pinch of salt

250 ml/8 fl oz/1 cup buttermilk

Rub the lard into the flour, bicarbonate of soda, cream of tartar and salt until the mixture resembles breadcrumbs. Stir in the milk and mix to a soft dough. Roll out on a lightly floured surface to 1 cm/½ in thick and cut out with a biscuit (cookie) cutter. Place the biscuits (crackers) on a greased baking (cookie) sheet and bake in a preheated oven at 230°C/450°F/gas mark 8 for 10 minutes until golden.

Tomato and Parmesan Pinwheels

Makes 16

225 g/8 oz Puff Pastry

30 ml/2 tbsp tomato purée (paste)

100 g/4 oz/1 cup Parmesan cheese, grated

Salt and freshly ground black pepper

Roll out the pastry (paste) to about 5 mm/¼ in thick. Spread with the tomato purée, then sprinkle with the cheese and season with salt and pepper. Roll up the pastry into a long sausage shape, then cut into 1 cm/½ in slices and arrange on a dampened baking (cookie) sheet. Bake in a preheated oven at 220°C/ 425°F/gas mark 7 for about 10 minutes until puffed and golden.

Tomato and Herb Biscuits

Makes 12

225 g/8 oz/2 cups plain (all-purpose) flour

5 ml/1 tsp caster (superfine) sugar

2.5 ml/½ tsp salt

40 ml/2½ tbsp baking powder

100 g/4 oz/½ cup butter or margarine

30 ml/2 tbsp milk

30 ml/2 tbsp water

4 ripe tomatoes, skinned, seeded and chopped

45 ml/3 tbsp chopped fresh basil

Mix together the flour, sugar, salt and baking powder. Rub in the butter or margarine until the mixture resembles breadcrumbs. Stir in the milk, water, tomatoes and basil and mix to a soft dough. Knead for a few seconds on a lightly floured surface, then roll out to 2.5 cm/1 in thick and cut into rounds with a biscuit (cookie) cutter. Place the biscuits well apart on a greased baking (cookie) sheet and bake in a preheated oven at 230°C/425°F/gas mark 7 for 15 minutes until puffed and golden.

Basic White Loaf

Makes three 450 g/1 lb loaves

25 g/1 oz fresh yeast or 40 ml/2½ tbsp dried yeast

10 ml/2 tsp sugar

900 ml/1½ pts/3¾ cups warm water

25 g/1 oz/2 tbsp lard (shortening)

1.5 kg/3 lb/12 cups strong plain (bread) flour

15 ml/1 tbsp salt

Blend the yeast with the sugar and a little of the warm water and leave in a warm place for 20 minutes until frothy. Rub the lard into the flour and salt, then stir in the yeast mixture and enough of the remaining water to mix to a firm dough that leaves the sides of the bowl cleanly. Knead on a lightly floured surface or in a processor until elastic and no longer sticky. Place the dough in an oiled bowl, cover with oiled clingfilm (plastic wrap) and leave in a warm place for about 1 hour until doubled in size and springy to the touch.

Knead the dough again until firm, divide into three and place in greased 450 g/1 lb loaf tins (pans) or shape into the loaves of your choice. Cover and leave to rise in a warm place for about 40 minutes until the dough reaches just above the top of the tins.

Bake in a preheated oven at 230°C/ 450°F/gas mark 8 for 30 minutes until the loaves begin to shrink away from the sides of the tins and are golden and firm, and hollow-sounding when tapped on the base.

Bagels

Makes 12

15 g/½ oz fresh yeast or 20 ml/ 4 tsp dried yeast

5 ml/1 tsp caster (superfine) sugar

300 ml/½ pt/1¼ cups warm milk

50 g/2 oz/¼ cup butter or margarine

450 g/1 lb/4 cups strong plain (bread) flour

A pinch of salt

1 egg yolk

30 ml/2 tbsp poppy seeds

Blend the yeast with the sugar and a little of the warm milk and leave in a warm place for 20 minutes until frothy. Rub the butter or margarine into the flour and salt and make a well in the centre. Add the yeast mixture, the remaining warm milk and the egg yolk and mix to a smooth dough. Knead until the dough is elastic and no longer sticky. Place in an oiled bowl, cover with oiled clingfilm (plastic wrap) and leave in a warm place for about 1 hour until doubled in size.

Knead the dough lightly, then cut it into 12 pieces. Roll each one into a long strip about 15 cm/6 in long and twist into a ring. Place on a greased baking (cookie) sheet, cover and leave to rise for 15 minutes.

Bring a large pan of water to the boil, then turn down the heat to a simmer. Drop a ring into the simmering water and cook for 3 minutes, turning once, then remove and place on a baking (cookie) sheet. Continue with the remaining bagels. Sprinkle the bagels with poppy seeds and bake in a preheated oven at 230°C/450°F/gas mark 8 for 20 minutes until golden.

Baps

Makes 12

25 g/1 oz fresh yeast or 40 ml/ 2½ tbsp dried yeast

5 ml/1 tsp caster (superfine) sugar

150 ml/¼ pt/2/3 cup warm milk

50 g/2 oz/¼ cup lard (shortening)

450 g/1 lb/4 cups strong plain (bread) flour

5 ml/1 tsp salt

150 ml/¼ pt/2/3 cup warm water

Blend the yeast with the sugar and a little of the warm milk and leave in a warm place for 20 minutes until frothy. Rub the lard into the flour, then stir in the salt and make a well in the centre. Add the yeast mixture, the remaining milk and the water and mix to a soft dough. Knead until elastic and no longer sticky. Place in an oiled bowl and cover with oiled clingfilm (plastic wrap). Leave in a warm place for about 1 hour until doubled in size.

Shape the dough into 12 flat rolls and arrange on a greased baking (cookie) sheet. Leave to rise for 15 minutes.

Bake in a preheated oven at 230°C/ 450°F/gas mark 8 for 15–20 minutes until well risen and golden.

Creamy Barley Loaf

Makes one 900 g/2 lb loaf

15 g/½ oz fresh yeast or 20 ml/4 tsp dried yeast

A pinch of sugar

350 ml/12 fl oz/1½ cups warm water

400 g/14 oz/3½ cups strong plain (bread) flour

175 g/6 oz/1½ cups barley flour

A pinch of salt

45 ml/3 tbsp single (light) cream

Blend the yeast with the sugar and a little of the warm water and leave in a warm place for 20 minutes until frothy. Mix the flours and salt in a bowl, add the yeast mixture, the cream and remaining water and mix to a firm dough. Knead until smooth and no longer sticky. Place in an oiled bowl, cover with oiled clingfilm (plastic wrap) and leave in a warm place for about 1 hour until doubled in size.

Knead again lightly, then shape into a greased 900 g/2 lb loaf tin (pan), cover and leave in a warm place for 40 minutes until the dough has risen above the top of the tin.

Bake in a preheated oven at 220°C/ 425°F/gas mark 7 for 10 minutes, then reduce the oven temperature to 190°C/375°F/gas mark 5 and bake for a further 25 minutes until golden brown and hollow-sounding when tapped on the base.

Beer Bread

Makes one 900 g/2 lb loaf

450 g/1 lb/4 cups self-raising (self-rising) flour

5 ml/1 tsp salt

350 ml/12 fl oz/1½ cups lager

Mix together the ingredients to a smooth dough. Shape into a greased 900 g/2 lb loaf tin (pan), cover and leave to rise in a warm place for 20 minutes. Bake in a preheated oven at 190°C/375°F/gas mark 5 for 45 minutes until golden brown and hollow-sounding when tapped on the base.

Boston Brown Bread

Makes three 450 g/1 lb loaves

100 g/4 oz/1 cup rye flour

100 g/4 oz/1 cup cornmeal

100 g/4 oz/1 cup wholemeal (wholewheat) flour

5 ml/1 tsp bicarbonate of soda (baking soda)

5 ml/1 tsp salt

250 g/9 oz/¾ cup black treacle (molasses)

500 ml/16 fl oz/2 cups buttermilk

175 g/6 oz/1 cup raisins

Mix together the dry ingredients, then stir in the treacle, buttermilk and raisins and mix to a soft dough. Spoon the mixture into three greased 450 g/1 lb pudding basins, cover with greaseproof (waxed) paper and foil and tie with string to seal the tops. Place in a large pan and fill with enough hot water to come half- way up the sides of the bowls. Bring the water to the boil, cover the pan and simmer for 2½ hours, topping up with boiling water as necessary. Remove the bowls from the pan and leave to cool slightly. Serve warm with butter.

Bran Flowerpots

Makes 3

25 g/1 oz fresh yeast or 40 ml/ 2½ tbsp dried yeast

5 ml/1 tsp sugar

600 ml/1 pt/2½ cups lukewarm water

675 g/1½ lb/6 cups wholemeal (wholewheat) flour

25 g/1 oz/¼ cup soya flour

5 ml/1 tsp salt

50 g/2 oz/1 cup bran

Milk to glaze

45 ml/3 tbsp cracked wheat

You will need three clean, new 13 cm/ 5 in clay flowerpots. Grease them well and bake in a hot oven for 30 minutes to prevent them from cracking.

Blend the yeast with the sugar and a little of the warm water and leave to stand until frothy. Mix the flours, salt and bran and make a well in the centre. Mix in the warm water and yeast mixture and knead to a firm dough. Turn out on to a floured surface and knead for about 10 minutes until smooth and elastic. Alternatively, you can do this in a food processor. Place the dough in a clean bowl, cover with oiled clingfilm (plastic wrap) and leave in a warm place to rise for about 1 hour until doubled in size.

Turn out on to a floured surface and knead again for 10 minutes. Shape into the three greased flowerpots, cover and leave to prove for 45 minutes until the dough has risen above the top of the pots.

Brush the dough with milk and sprinkle with the cracked wheat. Bake in a preheated oven at 230°C/450°F/gas mark 8 for 15 minutes. Reduce the oven temperature to 200°C/400°F/gas mark 6 and bake for a further 30 minutes until well risen and firm. Turn out and leave to cool.

Buttered Rolls

Makes 12

450 g/1 lb Basic White Loaf dough

100 g/4 oz/½ cup butter or margarine, diced

Make the bread dough and leave it to rise until doubled in size and springy to the touch.

Knead the dough again and work in the butter or margarine. Shape into 12 rolls and place them well apart on a greased baking (cookie) sheet. Cover with oiled clingfilm (plastic wrap) and leave to rise in a warm place for about 1 hour until doubled in size.

Bake in a preheated oven at 230°C/ 450°F/gas mark 8 for 20 minutes until golden brown and hollow-sounding when tapped on the base.

Buttermilk Loaf

Makes one 675 g/1½ lb loaf

450 g/1 lb/4 cups plain (all-purpose) flour

5 ml/1 tsp cream of tartar

5 ml/1 tsp bicarbonate of soda (baking soda)

250 ml/8 fl oz/1 cup buttermilk

Mix together the flour, cream of tartar and bicarbonate of soda in a bowl and make a well in the centre. Stir in enough of the buttermilk to mix to a soft dough. Shape into a round and place on a greased baking (cookie) sheet. Bake in a preheated oven at 220°C/425°F/gas mark 7 for 20 minutes until well risen and golden brown.

Canadian Corn Bread

Makes one 23 cm/9 in loaf

150 g/5 oz/1¼ cups plain (all-purpose) flour

75 g/3 oz/¾ cup cornmeal

15 ml/1 tbsp baking powder

2.5 ml/½ tsp salt

100 g/4 oz/1/3 cup maple syrup

100 g/4 oz/½ cup lard (shortening), melted

2 eggs, beaten

Mix together the dry ingredients, then blend in the syrup, lard and eggs and stir until well mixed. Spoon into a greased 23 cm/9 in baking tin (pan) and bake in a preheated oven at 220°C/425°F/gas mark 7 for 25 minutes until well risen and golden brown, and beginning to shrink away from the sides of the tin.

Cornish Rolls

Makes 12

25 g/1 oz fresh yeast or 40 ml/2½ tbsp dried yeast

15 ml/1 tbsp caster (superfine) sugar

300 ml/½ pt/1¼ cups warm milk

50 g/2 oz/¼ cup butter or margarine

450 g/1 lb/4 cups strong plain (bread) flour

A pinch of salt

Blend the yeast with the sugar and a little of the warm milk and leave in a warm place for 20 minutes until frothy. Rub the butter or margarine into the flour and salt and make a well in the centre. Add the yeast mixture and the remaining milk and mix to a soft dough. Knead until elastic and no longer sticky. Place in an oiled bowl and cover with oiled clingfilm (plastic wrap). Leave in a warm place for about 1 hour until doubled in size.

Shape the dough into 12 flat rolls and arrange on a greased baking (cookie) sheet. Cover with oiled clingfilm and leave to rise for 15 minutes.

Bake in a preheated oven at 230°C/ 450°F/gas mark 8 for 15–20 minutes until well risen and golden.

Country Flat Bread

Makes six small breads

10 ml/2 tsp dried yeast

15 ml/1 tbsp clear honey

120 ml/4 fl oz/½ cup warm water

350 g/12 oz/3 cups strong plain (bread) flour

5 ml/1 tsp salt

50 g/2 oz/¼ cup butter or margarine

5 ml/1 tsp caraway seeds

5 ml/1 tsp ground coriander

5 ml/1 tsp ground cardamom

120 ml/4 fl oz/½ cup warm milk

60 ml/4 tbsp sesame seeds

Blend the yeast and honey with 45 ml/3 tbsp of the warm water and 15 ml/1 tbsp of the flour and leave for about 20 minutes in a warm place until frothy. Mix the remaining flour with the salt, then rub in the butter or margarine and stir in the caraway seeds, coriander and cardamom and make a well in the centre. Mix in the yeast mixture, the remaining water and enough of the milk to make a smooth dough. Knead well until firm and no longer sticky. Place in an oiled bowl, cover with oiled clingfilm (plastic wrap) and leave in a warm place for about 30 minutes until doubled in size.

Knead the dough again, then shape into flat cakes. Place on a greased baking (cookie) sheet and brush with milk. Sprinkle with sesame seeds. Cover with oiled clingfilm and leave to rise for 15 minutes.

Bake in a preheated oven at 200°C/ 400°F/gas mark 6 for 30 minutes until golden.

Country Poppyseed Plait

Makes one 450 g/1 lb loaf

275 g/10 oz/2½ cups plain (all-purpose) flour

25 g/1 oz/2 tbsp caster (superfine) sugar

5 ml/1 tsp salt

10 ml/2 tsp easy-blend dried yeast

175 ml/6 fl oz/¾ cup milk

25 g/1 oz/2 tbsp butter or margarine

1 egg

A little milk or egg white for glazing

30 ml/2 tbsp poppy seeds

Mix together the flour, sugar, salt and yeast. Warm the milk with the butter or margarine, then mix into the flour with the egg and knead to a stiff dough. Knead until elastic and no longer sticky. Place in an oiled bowl, cover with oiled clingfilm (plastic wrap) and leave in a warm place for about 1 hour until doubled in size.

Knead again and shape into three sausage shapes about 20 cm/8 in long. Moisten one end of each strip and press them together, then plait the strips together, moisten and seal the ends. Place on a greased baking (cookie) sheet, cover with oiled clingfilm and leave to rise for about 40 minutes until doubled in size.

Brush with milk or egg white and sprinkle with poppy seeds. Bake in a preheated oven at 190°C/375°F/gas mark 5 for about 45 minutes until golden brown.

Country Wholemeal Bread

Makes two 450 g/1 lb loaves

20 ml/4 tsp dried yeast

5 ml/1 tsp caster (superfine) sugar

600 ml/1 pt/2½ cups warm water

25 g/1 oz/2 tbsp vegetable fat (shortening)

800 g/1¾ lb/7 cups wholemeal (wholewheat) flour

10 ml/2 tsp salt

10 ml/2 tsp malt extract

1 egg, beaten

25 g/1 oz/¼ cup cracked wheat

Blend the yeast with the sugar and a little of the warm water and leave for about 20 minutes until frothy. Rub the fat into the flour, salt and malt extract and make a well in the centre. Stir in the yeast mixture and the remaining warm water and mix to a soft dough. Knead well until elastic and no longer sticky. Place in an oiled bowl, cover with oiled clingfilm (plastic wrap) and leave in a warm place for about 1 hour until doubled in size.

Knead the dough again and shape into two greased 450 g/1 lb loaf tins (pans). Leave to rise in a warm place for about 40 minutes until the dough rises just above the tops of the tins.

Brush the tops of the loaves generously with egg and sprinkle with cracked wheat. Bake in a preheated oven at 230°C/ 450°F/gas mark 8 for about 30 minutes until golden brown and hollow-sounding when tapped on the base.

Curry Plaits

Makes two 450 g/1 lb loaves

120 ml/4 fl oz/½ cup warm water

30 ml/2 tbsp dried yeast

225 g/8 oz/2/3 cup clear honey

25 g/1 oz/2 tbsp butter or margarine

30 ml/2 tbsp curry powder

675 g/1½ lb/6 cups plain (all-purpose) flour

10 ml/2 tsp salt

450 ml/¾ pt/2 cups buttermilk

1 egg

10 ml/2 tsp water

45 ml/3 tbsp flaked (slivered) almonds

Mix the water with the yeast and 5 ml/1 tsp of the honey and leave to stand for 20 minutes until frothy. Melt the butter or margarine, then stir in the curry powder and cook over a low heat for 1 minute. Stir in the remaining honey and remove from the heat. Place half the flour and the salt in a bowl and make a well in the centre. Add the yeast mixture, the honey mixture and the buttermilk and gradually add the remaining flour as you mix to a soft dough. Knead until smooth and elastic. Place in an oiled bowl, cover with oiled clingfilm and leave in a warm place for about 1 hour until doubled in size.

Knead again and divide the dough in half. Cut each piece into three and roll into 20 cm/8 in sausage shapes. Moisten one end of each strip and press together in two lots of three to seal. Plait the two sets of strips and seal the ends. Place on a greased baking (cookie) sheet, cover with oiled clingfilm (plastic wrap) and leave to rise for about 40 minutes until doubled in size.

Beat the egg with the water and brush over the loaves, then sprinkle with almonds. Bake in a preheated oven at 190°C/375°F/gas mark 5 for 40 minutes until golden brown and hollow-sounding when tapped on the base.

Devon Splits

Makes 12

25 g/1 oz fresh yeast or 40 ml/ 2½ tbsp dried yeast

5 ml/1 tsp caster (superfine) sugar

150 ml/¼ pt/2/3 cup warm milk

50 g/2 oz/¼ cup butter or margarine

450 g/1 lb/4 cups strong plain (bread) flour

150 ml/¼ pt/2/3 cup warm water

Blend the yeast with the sugar and a little warm milk and leave in a warm place for 20 minutes until frothy. Rub the butter or margarine into the flour and make a well in the centre. Add the yeast mixture, the remaining milk and the water and mix to a soft dough. Knead until elastic and no longer sticky. Place in an oiled bowl and cover with oiled clingfilm (plastic wrap). Leave in a warm place for about 1 hour until doubled in size.

Shape the dough into 12 flat rolls and arrange on a greased baking (cookie) sheet. Leave to rise for 15 minutes.

Bake in a preheated oven at 230°C/ 450°F/gas mark 8 for 15–20 minutes until well risen and golden brown.

Fruited Wheatgerm Bread

Makes one 900 g/2 lb loaf

225 g/8 oz/2 cups plain (all-purpose) flour

5 ml/1 tsp salt

5 ml/1 tsp bicarbonate of soda (baking soda)

5 ml/1 tsp baking powder

175 g/6 oz/1½ cups wheatgerm

100 g/4 oz/1 cup cornmeal

100 g/4 oz/1 cup rolled oats

350 g/12 oz/2 cups sultanas (golden raisins)

1 egg, lightly beaten

250 ml/8 fl oz/1 cup plain yoghurt

150 ml/¼ pt/2/3 cup black treacle (molasses)

60 ml/4 tbsp golden (light corn) syrup

30 ml/2 tbsp oil

Mix together the dry ingredients and the sultanas and make a well in the centre. Blend together the egg, yoghurt, treacle, syrup and oil, then stir into the dry ingredients and mix to a softish dough. Shape into a greased 900 g/2 lb loaf tin (pan) and bake in a preheated oven at 180°C/350°F/gas mark 4 for 1 hour until firm to the touch. Leave to cool in the tin for 10 minutes before turning out on to a wire rack to finish cooling.

Fruity Milk Plaits

Makes two 450 g/1 lb loaves

15 g/½ oz fresh yeast or 20 ml/ 4 tsp dried yeast

5 ml/1 tsp caster (superfine) sugar

450 ml/¾ pt/2 cups warm milk

50 g/2 oz/¼ cup butter or margarine

675 g/1½ lb/6 cups plain (all-purpose) flour

A pinch of salt

100 g/4 oz/2/3 cup raisins

25 g/1 oz/3 tbsp currants

25 g/1 oz/3 tbsp chopped mixed (candied) peel

Milk for glazing

Blend together the yeast with the sugar and a little of the warm milk. Leave to stand in a warm place for about 20 minutes until frothy. Rub the butter or margarine into the flour and salt, stir in the raisins, currants and mixed peel and make a well in the centre. Mix in the remaining warm milk and the yeast mixture and knead to a soft but not sticky dough. Place in an oiled bowl and cover with oiled clingfilm (plastic wrap). Leave in a warm place for about 1 hour until doubled in size.

Knead again lightly, then divide in half. Divide each half into three and roll into sausage shapes. Moisten one end of each roll and press three gently together, then plait the dough, moisten and seal the ends. Repeat with the other dough plait. Place on a greased baking (cookie) sheet, cover with oiled clingfilm (plastic wrap) and leave to rise for about 15 minutes.

Brush with a little milk, then bake in a preheated oven at 200°C/400°F/gas mark 6 for 30 minutes until golden brown and hollow-sounding when tapped on the base.

Granary Bread

Makes two 900 g/2 lb loaves

25 g/1 oz fresh yeast or 40 ml/ 2½ tbsp dried yeast

5 ml/1 tsp honey

450 ml/¾ pt/2 cups warm water

350 g/12 oz/3 cups granary flour

350 g/12 oz/3 cups wholemeal (wholewheat) flour

15 ml/1 tbsp salt

15 g/½ oz/1 tbsp butter or margarine

Blend the yeast with the honey and a little of the warm water and leave in a warm place for about 20 minutes until frothy. Mix the flours and salt and rub in the butter or margarine. Blend in the yeast mixture and enough of the warm water to make a smooth dough. Knead on a lightly floured surface until smooth and no longer sticky. Place in an oiled bowl, cover with oiled clingfilm (plastic wrap) and leave in a warm place for about 1 hour until doubled in size.

Knead again and shape into two greased 900 g/2 lb loaf tins (pans). Cover with oiled clingfilm and leave to rise until the dough reaches to the top of the tins.

Bake in a preheated oven at 220°C/ 425°F/gas mark 7 for 25 minutes until golden brown and hollow-sounding when tapped on the base.

Granary Rolls

Makes 12

15 g/½ oz fresh yeast or 20 ml/ 2½ tbsp dried yeast

5 ml/1 tsp caster (superfine) sugar

300 ml/½ pt/1¼ cups warm water

450 g/1 lb/4 cups granary flour

5 ml/1 tsp salt

5 ml/1 tbsp malt extract

30 ml/2 tbsp cracked wheat

Blend the yeast with the sugar and a little of the warm water and leave in a warm place until frothy. Mix together the flour and salt, then blend in the yeast mixture, the remaining warm water and the malt extract. Knead on a lightly floured surface until smooth and elastic. Place in an oiled bowl, cover with oiled clingfilm (plastic wrap) and leave in a warm place for about 1 hour until doubled in size.

Knead lightly, then shape into rolls and place on a greased baking (cookie) sheet. Brush with water and sprinkle with cracked wheat. Cover with oiled clingfilm and leave in a warm place for about 40 minutes until doubled in size.

Bake in a preheated oven at 220°C/ 425°F/gas mark 7 for 10–15 minutes until hollow-sounding when tapped on the base.

Granary Bread with Hazelnuts

Makes one 900 g/2 lb loaf

15 g/½ oz fresh yeast or 20 ml/ 4 tsp dried yeast

5 ml/1 tsp soft brown sugar

450 ml/¾ pt/2 cups warm water

450 g/1 lb/4 cups granary flour

175 g/6 oz/1½ cups strong plain (bread) flour

5 ml/1 tsp salt

15 ml/1 tbsp olive oil

100 g/4 oz/1 cup hazelnuts, coarsely chopped

Blend the yeast with the sugar and a little of the warm water and leave in a warm place for 20 minutes until frothy. Mix together the flours and salt in a bowl, add the yeast mixture, the oil and the remaining warm water and mix to a firm dough. Knead until smooth and no longer sticky. Place in an oiled bowl, cover with oiled clingfilm (plastic wrap) and leave in a warm place for about 1 hour until doubled in size.

Knead again lightly and work in the nuts, then shape into a greased 900 g/2 lb loaf tin (pan), cover with oiled clingfilm and leave in a warm place for 30 minutes until the dough has risen above the top of the tin.

Bake in a preheated oven at 220°C/ 425°F/gas mark 7 for 30 minutes until golden brown and hollow-sounding when tapped on the base.

Grissini

Makes 12

25 g/1 oz fresh yeast or 40 ml/ 2½ tbsp dried yeast

15 ml/1 tbsp caster (superfine) sugar

120 ml/4 fl oz/½ cup warm milk

25 g/1 oz/2 tbsp butter or margarine

450 g/1 lb/4 cups strong plain (bread) flour

10 ml/2 tsp salt

Blend the yeast with 5 ml/1 tsp of the sugar and a little of the warm milk and leave in a warm place for 20 minutes until frothy. Melt the butter and remaining sugar in the remaining warm milk. Place the flour and salt in a bowl and make a well in the centre. Pour in the yeast and milk mixture and combine to make a moist dough. Knead until smooth. Place in an oiled bowl, cover with oiled clingfilm (plastic wrap) and leave in a warm place for about 1 hour until doubled in size.

Knead lightly, then divide into 12 and roll out into long, thin sticks and place, well apart, on a greased baking (cookie) sheet. Cover with oiled clingfilm and leave to rise in a warm place for 20 minutes.

Brush the bread sticks with water, then bake in a preheated oven at 220°C/425°F/ gas mark 7 for 10 minutes, then reduce the oven temperature to 180°C/350°F/ gas mark 4 and bake for a further 20 minutes until crisp.

Harvest Plait

Makes one 550 g/1¼ lb loaf

25 g/1 oz fresh yeast or 40 ml/ 2½ tbsp dried yeast

25 g/1 oz/2 tbsp caster (superfine) sugar

150 ml/¼ pt/2/3 cup warm milk

50 g/2 oz/¼ cup butter or margarine, melted

1 egg, beaten

450 g/1 lb/4 cups plain (all-purpose) flour

A pinch of salt

30 ml/2 tbsp currants

2.5 ml/½ tsp of ground cinnamon

5 ml/1 tsp grated lemon rind

Milk for glazing

Blend the yeast with 2.5 ml/½ tsp of the sugar and a little of the warm milk and leave in a warm place for about 20 minutes until frothy. Mix the remaining milk with the butter or margarine and leave to cool slightly. Mix in the egg. Place the remaining ingredients in a bowl and make a well in the centre. Stir in the milk and yeast mixtures and mix to a soft dough. Knead until elastic and no longer sticky. Place in an oiled bowl and cover with oiled clingfilm (plastic wrap). Leave in a warm place for about 1 hour until doubled in size.

Divide the dough into three and roll into strips. Moisten one end of each strip and seal the ends together, then plait them together and moisten and secure the other ends. Place on a greased baking (cookie) sheet, cover with oiled clingfilm and leave in a warm place for 15 minutes.

Brush with a little milk and bake in a preheated oven at 220°C/425°F/gas mark 7 for 15–20 minutes until golden brown and hollow-sounding when tapped on the base.

Milk Bread

Makes two 450 g/1 lb loaves

15 g/½ oz fresh yeast or 20 ml/ 4 tsp dried yeast

5 ml/1 tsp caster (superfine) sugar

450 ml/¾ pt/2 cups warm milk

50 g/2 oz/¼ cup butter or margarine

675 g/1½ lb/6 cups plain (all-purpose) flour

A pinch of salt

Milk for glazing

Blend the yeast with the sugar and a little of the warm milk. Leave to stand in a warm place for about 20 minutes until frothy. Rub the butter or margarine into the flour and salt and make a well in the centre. Mix in the remaining warm milk and the yeast mixture and knead to a soft but not sticky dough. Place in an oiled bowl and cover with oiled clingfilm (plastic wrap). Leave in a warm place for about 1 hour until doubled in size.

Knead again lightly, then divide the mixture between two greased 450 g/1 lb loaf tins (pans), cover with oiled clingfilm and leave to rise for about 15 minutes until the dough is just above the tops of the tins.

Brush with a little milk, then bake in a preheated oven at 200°C/400°F/gas mark 6 for 30 minutes until golden brown and hollow-sounding when tapped on the base.

Milk Fruit Loaf

Makes two 450 g/1 lb loaves

15 g/½ oz fresh yeast or 20 ml/ 4 tsp dried yeast

5 ml/1 tsp caster (superfine) sugar

450 ml/¾ pt/2 cups warm milk

50 g/2 oz/¼ cup butter or margarine

675 g/1½ lb/6 cups plain (all-purpose) flour

A pinch of salt

100 g/4 oz/2/3 cup raisins

Milk for glazing

Blend the yeast with the sugar and a little of the warm milk. Leave to stand in a warm place for about 20 minutes until frothy. Rub the butter or margarine into the flour and salt, stir in the raisins and make a well in the centre. Mix in the remaining warm milk and the yeast mixture and knead to a soft but not sticky dough. Place in an oiled bowl and cover with oiled clingfilm (plastic wrap). Leave in a warm place for about 1 hour until doubled in size.

Knead again lightly, then divide the mixture between two greased 450 g/1 lb loaf tins (pans), cover with oiled clingfilm and leave to rise for about 15 minutes until the dough is just above the tops of the tins.

Brush with a little milk, then bake in a preheated oven at 200°C/400°F/gas mark 6 for 30 minutes until golden brown and hollow-sounding when tapped on the base.

Morning Glory Bread

Makes two 450 g/1 lb loaves

100 g/4 oz/1 cup whole wheat grains

15 ml/1 tbsp malt extract

450 ml/¾ pt/2 cups warm water

25 g/1 oz fresh yeast or 40 ml/ 2½ tbsp dried yeast

30 ml/2 tbsp clear honey

25 g/1 oz/2 tbsp vegetable fat (shortening)

675 g/1½ lb/6 cups wholemeal (wholewheat) flour

25 g/1 oz/¼ cup milk powder (non-fat dry milk)

5 ml/1 tsp salt

Soak the whole wheat grains and malt extract in the warm water overnight.

Blend the yeast with a little more warm water and 5 ml/1 tsp of the honey. Leave in a warm place for about 20 minutes until frothy. Rub the fat into the flour, milk powder and salt and make a well in the centre. Stir in the yeast mixture, the remaining honey and the wheat mixture and mix to a dough. Knead well until smooth and no longer sticky. Place in an oiled bowl, cover with oiled clingfilm (plastic wrap) and leave in a warm place for about 1 hour until doubled in size.

Knead the dough again, then shape into two greased 450 g/1 lb loaf tins (pans). Cover with oiled clingfilm and leave in a warm place for 40 minutes until the dough reaches just above the tops of the tins.

Bake in a preheated oven at 200°C/ 425°F/gas mark 7 for about 25 minutes until well risen and hollow-sounding when tapped on the base.

Muffin Bread

Makes two 900 g/2 lb loaves

300 g/10 oz/2½ cups wholemeal (wholewheat) flour

300 g/10 oz/2½ cups plain (all-purpose) flour

40 ml/2½ tbsp dried yeast

15 ml/1 tbsp caster (superfine) sugar

10 ml/2 tsp salt

500 ml/17 fl oz/2¼ cups lukewarm milk

2.5 ml/½ tsp bicarbonate of soda (baking soda)

15 ml/1 tbsp warm water

Mix the flours together. Measure 350 g/12 oz/3 cups of the mixed flours into a bowl and mix in the yeast, sugar and salt. Stir in the milk and beat to a stiff mixture. Mix together the bicarbonate of soda and water and stir into the dough with the remaining flour. Divide the mixture between two greased 900 g/2 lb loaf tins (pans), cover and leave to rise for about 1 hour until doubled in size.

Bake in a preheated oven at 190°C/ 375°F/gas mark 5 for 1¼ hours until well risen and golden brown.

No-rise Bread

Makes one 900 g/2 lb loaf

450 g/1 lb/4 cups wholemeal (wholewheat) flour

175 g/6 oz/1½ cups self-raising (self-rising) flour

5 ml/1 tsp salt

30 ml/2 tbsp caster (superfine) sugar

450 ml/¾ pt/2 cups milk

20 ml/4 tsp vinegar

30 ml/2 tbsp oil

5 ml/1 tsp bicarbonate of soda (baking soda)

Mix together the flours, salt and sugar and make a well in the centre. Beat together the milk, vinegar, oil and bicarbonate of soda, pour into the dry ingredients and blend to a smooth dough. Shape into a greased 900 g/2 lb loaf tin (pan) and bake in a preheated oven at 180°C/350°F/gas mark 4 for 1 hour until golden brown and hollow-sounding when tapped on the base.

Pizza Dough

Makes enough for two 23 cm/9 in pizzas

15 g/½ oz fresh yeast or 20 ml/ 4 tsp dried yeast

A pinch of sugar

250 ml/8 fl oz/1 cup warm water

350 g/12 oz/3 cups plain (all-purpose) flour

A pinch of salt

30 ml/2 tbsp olive oil

Blend the yeast with the sugar and a little of the warm water and leave in a warm place for 20 minutes until frothy. Blend into the flour with the salt and olive oil and knead until smooth and no longer sticky. Place in an oiled bowl, cover with oiled clingfilm (plastic wrap) and leave in a warm place for 1 hour until doubled in size. Knead again and shape as required.

Oatmeal Cob

Makes one 450 g/1 lb loaf

25 g/1 oz fresh yeast or 40 ml/ 2½ tbsp dried yeast

5 ml/1 tsp caster (superfine) sugar

150 ml/¼ pt/2/3 cup lukewarm milk

150 ml/¼ pt/2/3 cup lukewarm water

400 g/14 oz/3½ cups strong plain (bread) flour

5 ml/1 tsp salt

25 g/1 oz/2 tbsp butter or margarine

100 g/4 oz/1 cup medium oatmeal

Blend the yeast and sugar with the milk and water and leave in a warm place until frothy. Mix together the flour and salt, then rub in the butter or margarine and stir in the oatmeal. Make a well in the centre, pour in the yeast mixture and mix to a soft dough. Turn out on a floured surface and knead for 10 minutes until smooth and elastic. Place in an oiled bowl, cover with oiled clingfilm (plastic wrap) and leave in a warm place to rise for about 1 hour until doubled in size.

Knead the dough again, then shape into a loaf shape of your choice. Place on a greased baking (cookie) sheet, brush with a little water, cover with oiled clingfilm and leave in a warm place for about 40 minutes until doubled in size.

Bake in a preheated oven at 230°C/ 450°F/gas mark 8 for 25 minutes until well risen and golden brown and hollow-sounding when tapped on the base.

Oatmeal Farl

Makes 4

25 g/1 oz fresh yeast or 40 ml/ 2½ tbsp dried yeast

5 ml/1 tsp honey

300 ml/½ pt/1¼ cups warm water

450 g/1 lb/4 cups strong plain (bread) flour

50 g/2 oz/½ cup medium oatmeal

2.5 ml/½ tsp baking powder

A pinch of salt

25 g/1 oz/2 tbsp butter or margarine

Blend the yeast with the honey and a little of the warm water and leave in a warm place for 20 minutes until frothy.

Mix together the flour, oatmeal, baking powder and salt and rub in the butter or margarine. Stir in the yeast mixture and the remaining warm water and mix to a medium-soft dough. Knead until elastic and no longer sticky. Place in an oiled bowl, cover with oiled clingfilm (plastic wrap) and leave in a warm place for about 1 hour until doubled in size.

Knead again lightly and shape into a round about 3 cm/1¼ in thick. Cut across into quarters and place, slightly apart but still in the original round shape, on a greased baking (cookie) sheet. Cover with oiled clingfilm and leave to rise for about 30 minutes until doubled in size.

Bake in a preheated oven at 200°C/ 400°F/gas mark 6 for 30 minutes until golden brown and hollow-sounding when tapped on the base.

Pitta Bread

Makes 6

15 g/½ oz fresh yeast or 20 ml/ 4 tsp dried yeast

5 ml/1 tsp caster (superfine) sugar

300 ml/½ pt/1¼ cups warm water

450 g/1 lb/4 cups strong plain (bread) flour

5 ml/1 tsp salt

Blend together the yeast, sugar and a little of the warm water and leave in a warm place for 20 minutes until frothy. Blend the yeast mixture and remaining warm water into the flour and salt and mix to a firm dough. Knead until smooth and elastic. Place in an oiled bowl, cover with oiled clingfilm (plastic wrap) and leave in a warm place for about 1 hour until doubled in size.

Knead again and divide into six pieces. Roll into ovals about 5 mm/¼ in thick and place on a greased baking (cookie) sheet. Cover with oiled clingfilm and leave to rise for 40 minutes until doubled in size.

Bake in a preheated oven at 230°C/ 450°F/gas mark 8 for 10 minutes until lightly golden.

Quick Brown Bread

Makes two 450 g/1 lb loaves

15 g/½ oz fresh yeast or 20 ml/ 4 tsp dried yeast

300 ml/½ pt/1¼ cups warm milk and water mixed

15 ml/1 tbsp black treacle (molasses)

225 g/8 oz/2 cups wholemeal (wholewheat) flour

225 g/8 oz/2 cups plain (all-purpose) flour

10 ml/2 tsp salt

25 g/1 oz/2 tbsp butter or margarine

15 ml/1 tbsp cracked wheat

Blend the yeast with a little warm milk and water and the treacle and leave in a warm place until frothy. Mix the flours and salt and rub in the butter or margarine. Make a well in the centre and pour in the yeast mixture, blending to a firm dough. Turn out on to a floured surface and knead for 10 minutes until smooth and elastic, or process in a food processor. Shape into two loaves and place in greased and lined 450 g/1 lb loaf tins (pans). Brush the tops with water and sprinkle with the cracked wheat. Cover with oiled clingfilm (plastic wrap) and leave in a warm place for about 1 hour until doubled in size.

Bake in a preheated oven at 240°C/ 475°F/gas mark 8 for 40 minutes until the loaves sound hollow when tapped on the base.

Moist Rice Bread

Makes one 900 g/2 lb loaf

75 g/3 oz/1/3 cup long-grain rice

15 g/½ oz fresh yeast or 20 ml/ 4 tsp dried yeast

A pinch of sugar

250 ml/8 fl oz/1 cup warm water

550 g/1¼ lb/5 cups strong plain (bread) flour

2.5 ml/½ tsp salt

Measure the rice into a cup, then pour into a pan. Add three times the volume of cold water, bring to the boil, cover and simmer for about 20 minutes until the water has been absorbed. Meanwhile blend the yeast with the sugar and a little of the warm water and leave in a warm place for 20 minutes until frothy.

Place the flour and salt in a bowl and make a well in the centre. Blend in the yeast mixture and the warm rice and mix to a soft dough. Place in an oiled bowl, cover with oiled clingfilm (plastic wrap) and leave in a warm place for about 1 hour until doubled in size.

Knead lightly, adding a little more flour if the dough is too soft to work, and shape into a greased 900 g/2 lb loaf tin (pan). Cover with oiled clingfilm and leave in a warm place for 30 minutes until the dough has risen above the top of the tin.

Bake in a preheated oven at 230°C/ 450°F/gas mark 8 for 10 minutes, then reduce the oven temperature to 200°C/ 400°F/gas mark 6 and bake for a further 25 minutes until golden brown and hollow-sounding when tapped on the base.

Rice and Almond Loaf

Makes one 900 g/2 lb loaf

175 g/6 oz/¾ cup butter or margarine, softened

175 g/6 oz/¾ cup caster (superfine) sugar

3 eggs, lightly beaten

100 g/4 oz/1 cup strong plain (bread) flour

5 ml/1 tsp baking powder

A pinch of salt

100 g/4 oz/1 cup ground rice

50 g/2 oz/½ cup ground almonds

15 ml/1 tbsp warm water

Cream together the butter or mar-garine and sugar until light and fluffy. Gradually beat in the eggs, then fold in the dry ingredients and the water to make a smooth dough. Shape into a greased 900 g/2 lb loaf tin (pan) and bake in a preheated oven at 180°C/350°F/gas mark 4 for 1 hour until golden brown and hollow-sounding when tapped on the base.

www.ingramcontent.com/pod-product-compliance
Lightning Source LLC
Chambersburg PA
CBHW071819080526
44589CB00012B/858